TH PRACTICAL HORSESHOER.

BEING A COLLECTION OF ARTICLES ON HORSESHOEING, IN ALL ITS BRANCHES, WHICH HAVE APPEARED FROM TIME TO TIME IN THE COLUMNS OF "THE BLACKSMITH AND WHEEL-WRIGHT" INCLUDING A CHAPTER ON HORSE PHYSIOGNOMY AND ANOTHER ON OX SHOEING.

COMPILED AND EDITED BY

M. T. RICHARDSON.

PROFUSELY ILLUSTRATED.

NEW YORK:
M. T. RICHARDSON, PUBLISHER.
1890.

JOHNSON BOOKS: BOULDER

This facsimile edition, first published in 1991, is an unabridged
reprint of the 1890 edition.

ISBN 1-55566-080-0

LCCCN 91-60936

Cover design by Molly Gough

Printed in the United States of America by
Johnson Publishing Company
1880 South 57th Court
Boulder, Colorado 80301

CONTENTS.

CONTENTS.

CHAPTER IX.

PREFACE.

Numerous works on horseshoeing have, from time to time, been published, but each one from the pen of a single individual and representing only his experience and theories as to the best methods of practice.

The present work embraces the varying views of a large number of horseshoers located in all parts of the United States, and as such is unique in its conception. The articles presented in the following pages have, many of them, been called out in response to the special inquiries of readers of *The Blacksmith and Wheelwright*, and all of them have previously appeared in the columns of that journal.

Nearly or quite every phase of this intricate subject is treated in some shape or other. At the risk of being accused by some shoers of presenting misleading views or incorrect methods, the Compiler has been liberal in making selections from the mass of matter which has appeared during the past ten years in the pages of *The Blacksmith and Wheelwright*. He has deemed it better to occasionally err in a selection rather than set himself up as a censor of practices which have been found to result satisfactorily in some hands, if not in all.

Each reader should judge for himself of the practicability of any given method before adopting it.

So many ways of accomplishing the same result are offered that it is confidently felt that at least one or more may be found to fit almost every conceivable case. Without desiring to disparage any other work on the same subject, the Editor feels that the present volume will be found invaluable to every man who shoes horses, wholly or in part, for a living.

Not by any means the least valuable feature of the present volume, will be found the numerous tools for horseshoers as well as devices for controlling unruly horses.

THE EDITOR.

THE PRACTICAL HORSESHOER.

INTRODUCTION.

The first method of protecting the horse's feet was by means of buskins, as they were termed ; then came a network, and lastly metal shoes. The impetuous action of the animals, their weight, and the angular form of the hoof have given much trouble about the manner of fastening on the shoes.

In Japan a kind of rushwork is used, which wraps the whole hoof, but it wears so fast on the road that travelers take a quantity with them on a journey, and poor people have them ready-made for sale at stopping places. The Mongols in high northern places shoe their horses with the palmy parts of reindeer horns.

In ancient Persia, where the breeds of gray, dun and bay racers are all hard-hoofed, the use of shoes in the sandy districts was needless, and not much attention was required to the abrasion of horn ; but in the higher and more stony districts, where the frog and edges of the hoof became more tender, it was looked to. In rapid and long-continued marches the hardest hoofed animals became crippled, and in history we find more than one instance where military expeditions were arrested in their progress until the horses had time to recover and restore their hoofs. These occurred chiefly when great operations were directed by foreign commanders who trusted to their energy for surmounting obstacles which native warriors believed to be impracticable. Thus Alexander the Great, at the siege of Cyzicus, was thwarted and delayed, while the Persians, under Darius, and the Parthians appear to have been equally distressed under similar circumstances.

At the time of Hannibal's invasion of the Roman Empire horseshoeing appears to have been unknown to the Carthaginians, as we read that that mighty warrior was sometimes compelled to give his famous cavalry horses a rest to enable their feet to recover from the soreness occasioned by rapid and prolonged marches. That the Arabs of the Hegira (A.D. 622), or within a generation later, shod their horses is plain, if we believe that the iron work on the summit of the standard of Hosién, at Ardbeil, was made from a horseshoe belonging to Abbas, uncle of Mohammed, by order of his daughter Fatima. It was brought, says the legend, from Arabia by Sheik Sofi. It is probable, therefore, that the art of shoeing must have been known among the Arabs as early as the time of Mohammed. These people say their first farrier came to them from the seaboard.

The greatest and earliest difficulty in the management of the horse's hoof seems to have been to combine a hard substance for the wear and tear with a ready means of fastening that would not injure the corneous substance, the ancients feeling that to make a puncture in the hoof would cause pain to the animal and otherwise injure him ; yet iron was found to be admissible. The form of the Asiatic horseshoe is circular, and instead of being fastened on by means of nails driven through the hoofs, it is secured by the clamps that appear to have closed on the outside or ascending surface. The exact counterpart of form, etc., existed at the period of the Ionian Greeks. The making of incisions in the hoof for the sharp points of the clamps to obtain a hold probably led to the knowledge that little or no pain was caused to the horse, and thus holes were bored for the nails, which became ever after the method of fastening.

BARBAROUS EXTRAVAGANCE.

The round horseshoe of old Arabian methods was an improvement on the Circassian, the outside clamps being omitted and nail holes substituted. Then came the alteration to thinner iron plates with but little opening. Then the more lengthened heels, all unfit for securing the feet in rocky countries. Then the war horses were shod with very large, heavy iron shoes, slightly turned up and pointed at the toe, also cocked at the heel with broad spikes· to afford a surer footing at a charge. In the chivalrous age a marching party of marauders, by placing the horses' shoes in a reversed manner, deceived pursuers, who, seeing the toe-marks in a given direction, turned their backs upon the route they pursued. This was practiced in the border wars by what were called " moss-troopers," who had often great reason to avoid capture, for the gallows not unfrequently closed their career.

Contrary to the general impression, says Gen. Dumas, the Arabs of the Sahara are in the habit of shoeing their horses with a view to the nature of the ground they are compelled to travel over. It seems to be the universal practice among these people to remove the shoes in spring, when the animals are turned out to grass, it being asserted that care must be taken not to check the renewal of the blood, which, it is thought, takes place at this season of the year. Their horseshoes are kept ready made (four sets of fore and hind shoes being a year's supply), and are fitted cold. The shoes are very light, but made of well-hammered iron. The hoof is allowed to grow freely, being neither pared nor shortened, the very stony ground and incessant work required of the horse sufficing to wear it off naturally, as by growth it projects over the iron.

The Arabian smith while plying his vocation sits with legs crossed and doubled under him.

The nails used are so constructed as to serve as calks, being provided with large oblong heads.

In the days when barbarous extravagance was taken for magnificence, a horse was occasionally shod with silver.

In the eleventh century—or, to give the exact date, A.D. 1038—Boniface, Marquis of Tuscany, a wealthy prince, in going to meet Beatrix, his intended bride, had his horses shod with silver, and the shoes were allowed to be cast off in order to be appropriated by the multitude that followed in throngs. At a later date Lord Doncaster, an English ambassador, acted in a similar manner on his public entry into Paris. The following account may be amusing: " Six trumpeters and two marshals in rich velvet liveries closely laced over with gold, led the way ; then came the ambassador and retinue of pages, booted, with horses richly caparisoned. The ambassador's horses were shod with silver shoes, lightly tacked on, and when he came to a place where persons of beauty or eminence were, his horses pranced and curveted in a showy manner and threw the shoes away, which the greedy multitude scrambled for, and he was content to be gazed on until a farrier—or, rather, argentier—from among his trained footmen took from out a velvet bag others and tacked them on, which lasted until he came to the next group of grandees, and thus, with much ado, he reached the Louvre."

William the Conqueror is said to have introduced horseshoeing in England, yet one Welbeck in Nottinghamshire, the property of a Saxon chief named Gamelbere, who retained his fief on the condition of shoeing the king's palfrey whenever he should lie at the Manor of Mansfield, and that he should give another palfrey whenever he should lame the king's animal, is recorded. If the account should be true, horseshoers must be older in England than the Norman Conquest, and when looking at the Bayeux tapestry it is perceived that both Saxon and Norman horses showed unequivocal marks of shoes and hob-nails on their feet.

Henry de Ferrers, who bore six horseshoes in his shield, was of the Norman invaders, and, it is believed, was intrusted with the inspection of the king's farriers. The armorial bearings are, it is true, older than the regular establishment of heraldry, but most likely they were, together with the family names, signs of office. The proper names of Marshall and Smith are singularly typified by hammers, tongs, anvils and horseshoes.

THE " CURVED CHARM."

In regard to the superstition attached to the " curved charm," it is universal. In Abyssinia, Barbary, and even in Guinea, horseshoes are fixed on doors and the thresholds of houses as much as in Europe, Asia and America. One is seen carved on a pagan Runic monument of the eleventh century, and the practice is known in Japan, China and Persia, and it is traced upon the cabin door of the Hottentot and the West Coast negro almost as frequently as on the barn door of a Dutch or English farmhouse. The horseshoe may be seen nailed to the mast of the coasting vessels, not after the manner of antiquity, with the heels up, but with the arch topmost. In Devonshire and Cornwall, England, they are nailed on the great west door of the church ; also on the door of the church at Halcomber, Devonshire, where formerly four horseshoes were seen, possibly to keep off witches, whose especial amusement it was

> "To untie the winds, and make them fight
> Against the churches."

Inquiry receives the same answer to symbolize a contemptible superstition in this country. Whittier says :

> " And still o'er many a neighbor's door
> She saw the horseshoe's curvéd charm."

> " The cautious goodman nails no more
> A horseshoe on his outside door,
> Lest some unseemly hag should fit
> To his own mouth her bridle bit.'

The shoe, an illustration (Fig. 1) of which is here given, was taken from the foot of one of the Arabian horses presented to General Grant by the Sultan of Turkey. According to Flem-

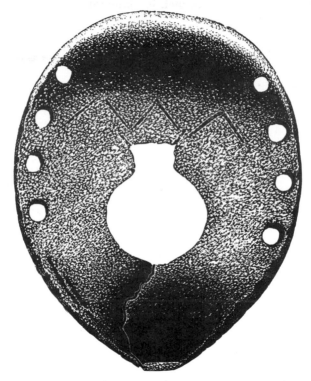

Fig. 1.—Shoe from the foot of one of the Arabian Stallions presented to General Grant in 1879 by the Sultan of Turkey.

ing, the horses of the East have been shod with similar shoes for the past 500 years, the only variation from the form shown in the engraving being in the opening for the frog, which is usually made triangular.

The dimensions of this shoe are as follows :   Length, $5\frac{3}{8}$

inches; width, 4¼ inches; thickness, ⅛ of an inch. The heel, which is bent up about ⅝ of an inch, shows a fracture in the iron at the point where it was originally welded. The nail-holes are one-fourth of an inch in diameter.

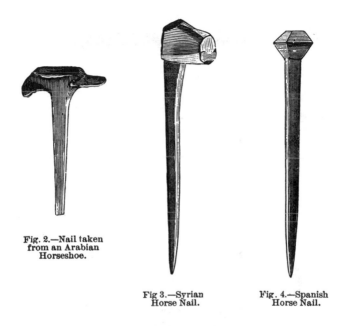

Fig. 2.—Nail taken from an Arabian Horseshoe.

Fig 3.—Syrian Horse Nail.

Fig. 4.—Spanish Horse Nail.

In Fig. 2 is shown the style of nail used in shoeing Arabian horses. It seems bungling and clumsy in comparison with the neat, trim American nails. Fig. 3 is, if anything, more bungling in construction than the Arabian nail, and represents the nail in use in Syria. Fig. 4, a Spanish nail, is a step forward, and, at least, resembles our modern nail.

CHAPTER I.

HORSES AND HORSESHOEING.

The Treatment of Horses.

Being very fond of horses, and finding in a good lively drive with an occasional friendly "brush" more of real solid enjoyment than in almost any other recreation, I am naturally led to think much upon the subject of the proper care and treatment of horses, and also through observation and comparison to form opinions as to suitable vehicles and best condition of roads, through the medium of which the most enjoyment may be had with the least of wear and tear and danger.

A horse fit to be called a good roadster, that is, one having the necessary amount of speed to start up and pull a wagon with two men over a country road, far from level, at a really rapid gait, must have some breeding, be in good health and condition, and have good feet. What are good strains of blood can be learned from breeders. There must be bone, and muscle, and proper form, but there must be intelligence and courage, with that gamecock pluck which cannot be found in dunghills. The right horses may be had by the thousand, and how to properly feed and care for them in general, covering all matters of stabling, ventilation, grooming, clothing, harness and fittings, how to drive to develop latent speed and improve upon that already developed, or at least to keep the developed trotter or roadster at the best, are subjects that have been so thoroughly treated upon by veterinarians, professional drivers, and gentlemen amateurs as to appear to leave nothing more to be said.

Still it is a fact that there are continually many of the most promising horses going wrong—"going all to pieces," to quote a common saying—in spite of being in the best of hands, where no reasonable trouble or expense would be counted too great whereby they could be kept right or cured after going wrong. These things show that either the teaching is at fault, or that little, seemingly unimportant conditions, so slight as to be overlooked, are really of great consequence.

A great many horses have a hitch in the gait produced by driving at speed too far when the pulling weight was great, or asking for a little too much speed of a colt. Asking the horse to speed right out before the proper amount of slow work has been done on first leaving the stable, produces the same defect. Hitching is nearly as bad as cribbing, is unsightly and annoying, and cuts speed down equal to absolute lameness. It is sometimes cured, but where one confirmed hitcher is taught to again go square, hundreds of square, pure-gaited horses might be kept so by "waiting a little."

From a condition of absolute soundness, feet get sore, get, in fact, in the same condition which is known to be the sequel of acute founder neglected, and still without any acute founder. Neglect of proper paring at reasonable intervals; lack of suitable exercise; want of necessary moisture ; ill-fitting shoes which, by preventing the foot from performing in all its parts the natural functions that tend to the secretion of healthy horn and the preservation through suitable action of proper shape; bruising of the sole by contact with small stones in driving, these stones being often picked up between the frog and web of the shoe and carried for miles, or even left in the foot for days by that class of men who say, "Humph, I never trouble myself about a horse's foot. If a horse is sound he wants nothing done to his feet"—these and divers other causes gradually—and to the owners and drivers many times—imperceptibly produce a condition of the feet which shortens the gait, impairs the speed, and causes on-lookers to say : "——'s horse is sore, actually goes lame at times"; and still the gentlest hint to the owner that his horse is not "all right" will be indignantly be met with the response, "Sound as any horse in the world," until downright lameness ensues. Now something must be done, and the veterinarian is consulted, who, with pills and powders, balls, blisters, and poultices, special shoeing and hoof ointment, soakers and bandages, and continuous care, palliates the horse's disease and depletes the pocket of the owner, and finally admits, when patience has been exhausted, what he knew was the fact in the beginning, that "all treatment is only palliative—a cure is impossible."

Well, what can be done? Much may be done. Insist upon having as much of the superfluous growth of hoof cut away at each shoeing as will relieve the foot from any undue pressure caused by excessive growth. Don't pare the frogs, but, by sufficient moisture, keep them in such condition that "frog pressure" shall come upon an elastic cushion, not upon a substance as unyielding as the wall itself. Pressure on the frog is beneficial *only* when the frog is in proper condition to receive it. Don't insist too strongly upon leaving the sole untouched by the knife without first knowing what sort of feet you are dealing with. Some feet will shed out the dead horn from the sole in scales of considerable thickness once in a month or six weeks, and never need to have the sole pared at all. Other feet which have the sole untouched by the knife will never shed out a particle of the sole for an entire year, and by the accumulation of hoof which should not remain, and if not shed should be cut out, such feet are subjected to pressure which must cause excessive pain and produce corns and sore, shortened action.

To compensate for the change from the cool, soft turf, with the morning dew upon the grass, and the occasional wade in the brook or through the marsh which the horse finds in pasturage, to the hard, dry roads, with the dust, heated in summer to blistering, and the dry, unyielding floor of the stable, there must be some moistening or softening agency applied to the feet at times or there will be contraction, corns, uncertain, tender-footed action, and finally downright lameness. "Yes, give them a good soaking out in hot water two or three times a week, and stuff them over night with linseed meal and wheat bran." No, not till such treatment is necessary, and with proper care it need not become necessary. Keep a soaking tub or box, and, with as much clean, cool water as will reach above the coronet, let the horse stand with fore-feet immersed for a few minutes, or an hour, once in a few days, or weeks, or every day, as the dryness of the roads or the condition of the particular feet in question demands. This, with the application of a good hoof ointment in some cases, will do much good. Aim to keep the feet cool, with the frogs in an elastic condition. Make a soaking box 18 inches long, 12 inches wide, and 7 inches deep inside, by having the sides the same length of the bottom, and nailing them to the bottom, then nailing the end pieces to the sides and bottom, the bottom board being inside. Such a box will hold water as well as a tub, is lighter, and takes up less room. Make it of pine from full 1 inch to 1¼ inches thick.

When a horse comes in from a drive, clean his feet out with some sensible kind of hoof-pick which will get the gravel from between the sole and web of the shoe, then with a sponge and pail of water wash each foot clean, inside and out. Of hoof ointments there are plenty. Vaseline will answer first-rate.

If a quick drive is to be made, whether of ten or twelve miles within the hour, or of twenty or thirty miles at the same rate, don't be in a hurry at the start. Begin easily, warm your horse up gradually, get the joints limbered up and in good working order, and as the lungs and heart get in proper action, with stomach and bowels relieved as they will be by waiting a little, your horse can rattle along easily at a rate which would have made him puff and blow, and scour, and lather if started out too fast at first, and you "get there" with your horse in good shape. With some drivers certain horses are said to be "poor feeders," while with other drivers the same horses will do as much work and never lose a feed. Don't start out too strong: always ease off a little toward the last end of a drive. Slackening down to a jog or walk for the last mile of a drive makes, sometimes, hours of difference in the time it takes for the horse to be dry and comfortable, besides letting the machinery, which has been working at its utmost tension, get back to something like its normal condition under easy action, instead of coming to a standstill from the high state of strain.

About Horseshoeing.

It is probable that on no other subject pertaining to mechanical practice is there more diversity of opinion. If we go to the authors of treatises on horseshoeing, we are told that to keep the horse's foot in a perfect condition of health it is simply necessary to shoe according to the rules laid down by them; but when we turn from the opinions expressed and rules laid down by one writer, to find him contradicted on every important point by other authorities, what are we to do? With one the all-important thing is "cold fitting," while another recommends "hot fitting," not simply as admissible and something to be tolerated, but as the only way in which a shoe can be properly fitted, and as being a positive benefit to the foot rather than an injury.

To open out the heels, even to drawing blood—using a saw for the purpose when necessity, or laziness, suggests it, and then cut down the wall all that it will bear, followiug this by a cutting away of the entire sole until it readily yields to slight pressure with the thumb, or till the blood oozes through, while the frog is also nicely trimmed off, is advised by one, while another says, "The frog and sole should never, under any circumstances, be cut at all."

But the subject is of too wide a scope, the opinions and practices of horseshoers and horse-owners differ too radically ; while the almost endless variety of feet to be shod, the variety multiplied over and over by the varied conditions in which the feet are fcund, owing in some measure to shoeing both good and bad, leave too much to be written to hope for more than the most casual reference here to a few of the abuses to be found.

How better point out these abuses, as they look to the writer, than to relate some scraps of personal experience? But need I put this experience in the first person? Have not so many other horse-owners been through the same experience that to state the fact, leaving out the "I," will come right home to them ? A new horse is purchased after careful examination of feet and limbs ; the gait and manner of going are all that could be desired, and there is not a mark on any ankle or knee to show that there has ever been such a thing as striking either forward or behind. For two, three, or even for four or five weeks the horse is driven with the same shoes he wore when purchased, the clinches get out so that it looks dangerous to go longer without shoeing, and still there has been no interfering. The horse is taken to the shop and has "a new set all round." The old shoes when removed are contemptuously tossed into the scrap heap, with the remark that "it is a great wonder that the horse could go at all with such things on; should suppose he would cut himself all to pieces." Now the horse is to be shod properly. No more great sprawling shoes.

The feet are cut down, the soles are pared thin, the frogs are "trimmed into some shape," and the shoes are fitted *full* on the outside and *close* on the inside. Of course there is no harm in fitting the shoe full even to projecting a little on the outside, but on the inside, where there may be danger of striking, the shoe must be fitted and nailed on *close*. What is close? Why, anywhere fron one-sixteenth to one-quarter of an inch out from being flush with the wall on the inside quarter, the projecting hoof to be rasped off after the shoe is nailed on and the clinches laid down. In rasping off the projecting wall from the inner quarter to the toe, the shoer, to avoid an unsightly joining of angles, carries the rasping up on the wall to, perhaps, within an inch, or thereabouts, of the coronet; and of course to make it look right the rasping must be continued all the way around to the same height, when by a liberal application of saliva, and a rub with the hand or corner of the apron, or sometimes with a dampened sponge kept for the purpose, the injury to the enamel is to some extent concealed temporarily, and the horse is pronounced well shod.

What is the result?

The small stones which strike the sole cause the horse to flinch and finally to go almost continually lame, or at least with an uncertain gait, caused in part by actual hurt and partly from fear of being hurt. There is a tendency of the ankles to turn in, and also of the knee, at each successive step, owing to the lessened amount of ground bearing which the foot has on its inner half. Half? No; too much has been cut away, and with the inequality of surface on which the foot must be placed in traveling the greater amount of surface covered by that portion of the foot outside of the frog than inside, the greater distance from the center out acting as a powerful lever, the ankles and knees are deflected inward so much as to make it impossible for the passing foot to get by without hitting.

Here we have an interfering horse, hitting every ankle and both knees as a direct, unmistakable result of shoeing ; and the worst of it is, from just the shoeing which is so generally believed to be a preventive of interfering, and which will be persisted in until the horse becomes a perfect cripple unless "booted all over," while the walls of such feet, denuded of the enamel, and at every shoeing losing more and more of their substance through the use of the rasp, will become so split as to make it difficult to find a sound place for a nail.

It is not cutting away the little which may be cut from the inside of the foot that insures its passing the ankle or knee without hitting, but it is the position of the knee or ankle relative to the line of motion of the foot in passing which has the greatest influence. Who says, "Everybody knows that" ? Who says, "That's just why we shoe in the way you condemn"? Well, then, tell me why this horse began to interfere almost from the moment he left your shop, and in driving ten miles had bloody ankles, laying the foundation for a callous spot on each ankle, where no hair will ever again grow, while he had not a mark of this kind before you took him in hand ?

Shoeing Horses.

Said a driver of trotting horses to the writer, in speaking of a valuable trotting mare which was beaten in straight heats three weeks ago: "When I took her, directly after the race, I found her feet so soft from having been stuffed with linseed meal that she actually could not go without flinching, and the smell from her feet was enough to knock one over."

Said I, " Did you not drive this mare yesterday against the same horse that beat her in straight heats three weeks ago?"

" I did," he replied, " and she won in three heats, under a good pull all the way, and is going now as sound as a colt. She wants no stuffing of feet; just ' tub her out ' once in a while. It doesn't do to keep a horse's feet too soft."

One writer says: " I have found more trouble caused by not cutting enough than by cutting too much; I like to see all dead tissue cut away."

Into just such hands a friend of mine fell who had a good road horse that could trot in about two-thirty, and a sound-going one she was, as sure-footed as a deer. Not long after the " cutting away of all dead tissue " began, this well-shod animal with good feet surprised her driver by falling down, and in the space of six months fell five or six times, while in traveling she often flinched as though her fore-feet were tender. "Stop cutting," said a man whose advice was asked. The cutting was stopped, except to cut from the wall enough at each shoeing to keep pace with the growth, leaving the sole untouched, and this valuable horse is just as good and sure-footed as ever again.

" Fitted with a bearing all around the wall except the heels," says this writer, and he continues: " George in shoeing a horse forward fitted the shoes lightly on the heel."

Now, there can be no more reprehensible practice in shoeing than this of fitting a shoe so that when nailed on, and drawn home and clinched, there is an open space between the shoe and the heels of all the way from one-sixteenth of an inch to a full quarter of an inch, this space growing less as it goes forward from the heel until finally at some point away around at the side of the foot the shoe bears.

I heard a blacksmith say, not long since, that "some men were cranks on horseshoeing." Perhaps I am one. I have, at least, decided opinions about this matter of a level bearing of the shoe all over the entire wall, and, above all, at the heel. I have many times seen that kind of fitting which would permit a case-knife to pass between the hoof and the shoe at a point from two to two and a half inches, and even three inches, forward from where the extreme point of the heel should have rested on the shoe, but did not touch it within an eighth of an inch, and in extreme cases an open space was shown of from three-sixteenths to one-quarter inch at the heel. It is often the case that this condition applies to the inner quarter and heel only, or, more correctly speaking, the opening is hardly ever alike as between the inside and outside quarter.

If the man who fits shoes thus is asked why he does it, he says, "That horse has corns, and by cutting away the hoof, wall, sole, and braces on the inside quarter it relieves the pressure." Yes, and produces an undue strain in the foot, as the weight is brought to bear at each step taken, or for every moment of time in which the horse stands. Lift a foot thus shod and note the space between hoof and shoe, and then, letting the foot rest on the ground or a level floor, let an assistant raise the other foot, thereby throwing the weight upon the foot under examination. Why! The shoe springs up to the foot! No, the foot springs down to the shoe. Well, anyhow, the space between is no longer to be seen; the foot rests on the shoe. Just here the man who puts the shoe on says: "Well, what do you want? It comes down as soon as the weight comes on it."

I want the shoe and foot both level, so that they come together evenly all the way around from toe to heel, and I don't want the man who pares the foot to shorten the bearing at the heel by cutting off that extreme back corner, which is done so dexterously by a turn of the wrist, and with such a mixture of profound satisfaction and malice aforethought.

If the weight thrown upon the foot tends to expand and produce action in the back part of the foot, varying in amount just as the weight brought to bear is greater or less, or as the impact is more or less violent as between walking and varying rates of speed up to the best gait, is it not plain that the best condition in which to place the foot is on a plain level bearing, and, further, is it not plain that this mischievous space between hoof and shoe must become, as the horse is driven, a receptacle for dirt and gravel, the bearing of which on the seat of corn cannot be otherwise than injurious? How would a man like it, I wonder, to wear a pair of boots with two-thirds of the length of the boot from the toes back strapped firmly to a bearing fitting the contour of that part of the foot, while back of this part of the foot was a depression in the insole of such magnitude that the heel could only reach any bearing by the foot springing out of its natural shape, the sole of the boot being made rigid? But, to complete the parallel, let us take off the counter from this boot, so that the dirt and gravel shall have free access to the bearing on which the heel must come if it bears at all. How would a man walk shod thus? His feet would soon be so sore that he would be afraid to put them to the ground, and any inequalities in the surface which caused this rigid sole to which his foot was strapped to be elevated at the heel, or turned to one side, or, in fact, the slightest deviation from a level plain bearing of these boots upon the ground, would cause additional pain. Shoe a horse as I have described, and watch his gait, and say whether the parallel is not complete. One shoeing has changed many a horse from an easy-gaited, sure-footed traveler to a tender-footed, uncertain-gaited stumbler that flinches every time the feet touch a stone or uneven spot in the road, until the ever-present dread of hurting the feet on the part of the horse destroys all pleasure on the part of the driver.

I am contradicting the authorities, I know, but I once had a horse shod for quarter cracks according to the popular idea, "Feet cut away to remove all pressure from the parts affected." It was a bad case, two cracks in each foot, both sides of both feet cracked. "Old Ben" went so lame that I was ashamed to drive him. I took him back after a few days to the man who had cut away his feet and shod him. I said:

"This horse can't go, so I want these shoes taken off, and his feet pared level; then I want a pair of good thick shoes of equal thickness all the way around put on so that they will bear evenly from toe to heel, the shoe and hoof coming together evenly all the way around just as any two level surfaces must; then when the weight is thrown upon the feet there will be no unequal strain set up."

Did P. K.—counted the best shoer in town—see the point? No, he did not. He said, "You can't pare those feet down enough now to make them level without paring too much; you will have to wait till they grow. Besides, if the feet could be pared and shod according to your idea you could not drive the horse at all. In fact, I don't believe you could get him home; you had better let him be as he is. I think, with my experience in horseshoeing, you ought to be willing to admit that my judgment is better on the subject than yours."

Said I: "The horse is mine; if he can't go after shoeing in my way he may stand still, and if you shoe him according to my instructions you shall take none of the blame if he is worse for it." The bar shoes were removed and carefully preserved by the shoer, who said: "You will want them again to-morrow." A pair of heavy plain shoes were put on which fitted " to a shaving." Old Ben started out without a semblance of lameness. I used him for a year and his feet grew out sound. He could pull two men to a top carriage in two-fifty, and his walking gait was five miles per hour. What a roadster he was ! How near he came to being ruined !—*By* S. W. G.

Practical Horseshoeing.

My experience in horseshoeing, which extends over quite a number of years, teaches me that there can be no arbitrary rules laid down by which we must work in shoeing horses.

There are as many different shapes of feet in horses as there are the human family, and as many different gaits, all of which require a different shoe and a different style of shoeing.

First, there is the draught horse, which usually has a large round hoof, and needs a strong, heavy shoe well chamfered out on the inside next to the sole. His foot in a state of health, in our climate, is nearly always very hard, so I take great pains in paring the sole. I do not cut out all the horn, as some do; I take out the dead sole, but do not pare so thin that I can spring it with my thumb nail, as I think that is too thin to prevent injury to the sole by stubs or stones, and will bring ice and snow in too close contact with the sensitive sole.

I make a shoe the shape of the foot and as large as I can nail on, bringing it around under the heel just sufficient to get a good bearing on the crust of the hoof, but not close enough to injure the frog. As much injury can be done by shoeing too wide as by shoeing too close at the heels.

I let the shoe extend back of the heels from three-eighths to one-half inch, and where they are calked I slant the calks

at the heels a little back and the toe calk a little forward.
Where the horse is kept on shoes all the time I use a toe clip;
but where he runs barefoot all the summer I consider a toe
clip a positive injury, as the hoof is very liable to crack where
clip sets in when the horse is turned barefoot in the summer
on our hard roads.

I use a nail as small as I dare, because it is less liable to
tear the hoof. I drive the nails well up into the hoof, which
I am able to do because the shoe is fully as large as the foot.
I clinch or draw them down very tightly, and, if the foot is
perfectly level, tight drawing will not do any harm. I cut
the clinches quite short and rasp them to an edge, but do
not cut into the nail with the corner of the rasp or cut a fur-
row into the hoof.

In clinching down I pound down the clinch with my hammer, being careful to strike equally down toward the head
of the nail, as if I were riveting it ; and if any of the nail
sticks out I rasp it off, but never try to drive it into the hoof
as a wrought nail is driven into a pine board, as that will
always loosen the shoe. I do as little rasping as possible,
believing it to be an injury to the hoof.

I always begin to nail at the toe and nail backward, as
this will expand the hoof ; and if the horse is hoof-bound,
by careful driving of the nails the hoof can be spread all the
horse needs or can stand. In this way I have cured several
cases of hoof-bound. It is much better than spreading the
shoe after nailing on.

In shoeing livery or buggy horses I use as light a shoe as
I can get. I make the calks, if any are required, very small
and short, and I file the shoe bright and smooth, and then file
the corner off the upper side, so that when it is on there is a
bright strip around the shoe next the foot about the size of
a No. 12 wire. This is a great improvement in the looks of
the foot. I generally fit a shoe hot, unless the owner objects,
as he sometimes does, but I only touch the foot with the

shoe enough to see where to cut to make a good, tight, level fit. I never burn the shoe into the hoof.

When a horse interferes, I pare the foot a little the lowest on the outside, turn the inside calk just as usual, weld a long calk on the outside line of the shoe, leaving it the full length, and place the toe calk a little to the inside of the center. This seldom fails to prevent striking where the leg is not swollen.

I have never made the shoeing of race horses a study as I have the shoeing of draught, livery, and stage horses.—*By* B. N. S.

Horseshoeing.

I have found, in my twenty-five years' experience in blacksmithing and horseshoeing, that no work comes in the shop that requires more care, thought, and investigation than horseshoeing.

The first thing to consider is preparing the foot for the shoe. I think there can be more harm done by doing too much at this stage of the job than in doing too little. But it is impossible to frame any rules that would be applicable to all feet, for the upright or arched foot requires very different treatment from that necessary for a flat foot with a low heel. In the arched foot the horn grows very fast, especially on the sole and towards the toe, and if the shoe has been on the foot for a considerable length of time it will be necessary to use the knife and rasp quite freely. But in the flat foot the horn grows very sparingly, and consequently the knife and rasp should be used with caution. In preparing the upright foot for the shoe, the dead horn should be removed from the sole first. It will usually come off in flakes and scales. When it has been removed, you will have a fair idea of how much should be taken from the wall. In all cases I think it best not to interfere much with the bars or the frog, for these are very important parts of the foot. Yet how often has a foot been contracted by the cutting away of these important parts! Then the smith will too often resort to some cruel mechanical device for opening the heels.

It has been said, with truth, that the nailing of an iron shoe on the foot of a living horse is an unnatural thing to do, but, as it must be done, let us, fellow-craftsmen, strive to do it in the most natural way possible. And to do this we must first get the foot as near as we can to its natural shape, and then make the shoe to fit the foot. Keep it full with the wall from the quarter to the heel, and I think it is very important that the shoe should bear only on the wall of the foot. Use as small a nail as possible and punch the holes large enough, so the nails will not bend in them. I would recommend punching the holes to suit the angle of the foot—that is, if the foot is an upright one, let the holes be almost through. But if the foot is flat, make the hole slant inwardly to suit the greater angle of the foot.—*By* W. M.

General Directions for Shoeing Horses.

In shoeing horses it is difficult to lay down a rule to apply to all cases. We find such a great difference in horses' feet, generally speaking. Even in single cases we find no two feet which should be shod exactly the same. In the first place, it is of great importance to the shoer to understand the nature of a horse's foot; then he can very easily tell when a foot is in a right position, or when it is misplaced. When he understands the different position of the bones, tendons, and ligaments, then he can very easily see where the foot needs trimming. Now, there is not attention enough given to this part of the trade of shoeing.

In trimming a horse's foot, of course it is necessary to

know which part is high and which is low. It would not do for me to say, "Trim all feet alike," because all feet are not alike. That is why I say there is not enough attention given to placing horses' feet in the right position. For instance, a horse comes to the shop, and the owner says: "This horse is lame and I want you to shoe him." The smith takes off the shoes, or sets his man at it, and tells him to pare the feet. He does so, and generally takes off as much in one place as in another. The smith then fits the shoes level, it is supposed, and they are driven on. The horse goes off better, perhaps, for a day or two, then it is the same trouble over again.

Perhaps the horse is high outside, which causes a misplaced position of the bones; then nature and the smith have a tug of war, and the smith generally comes out ahead, for, if the horse is not square on his feet, he certainly cannot go right. We ourselves cannot travel easy if we are traveling all on one side of our shoes, and it is just the same with a horse, except that the poor beast cannot tell in words where the sore spot is, so he takes the only course left for him—that is, to limp and hobble along.

Some owners of horses like to have their horse's feet cut, but a very little, especially the frog; but I have found more trouble caused by not cutting enough than by cutting too much. Some will say : "Cut the wall and not the sole," but you will find that by leaving too much sole it will leave your frog smaller—that is, it cuts off the supply of blood from the frog. Besides, too much frog checks the growth of the sole and other parts of the foot.

How often we find a large, prominent frog and very little sole, and that very dry and dead and chippy, no life, not enough blood to support and feed it. I like to see all dead tissue cut away. Then the live tissue has a chance to grow.

Of course nature intends the feet to be kept soft. The feet of horses that are kept on dry, hard floors, and work on pavements and dry roads, will get hard and dry. Now, I believe thoroughly in stuffing horses' feet. Some will ask what is the best thing to pack a horse's feet with. Some use moss and water, but I don't like it, as I find it makes a foot grow very fast but very thin, and consequently very weak. The best thing I know of for keeping the heat and fever out and grow a good solid foot is salt or marsh mud. If it cannot be got, take oil-meal or flaxseed meal and make a poultice. Put it on warm. Use it every night until you see a change, which will be before long. You will find that it will give your horse a great deal of comfort, besides saving a large amount of time which a smith has to spend in trying to trim, when it ought to take only a very little. Every horse owner who loves a good horse should look carefully after this matter, as a smith cannot trim a foot properly unless it is in a healthy condition.

Another important point in trimming is to commence early. This week I have seen two young colts trimmed, one nine and the other nineteen months old. They were both trimmed last fall, and the colt nine months old had the most perfect feet. Let a colt run until he is three years old, and you not only have imperfect feet, but you have a bad colt to shoe where you might have had a lamb for gentleness. They should get used to the shop and to having their feet handled. I have seen some colts, three and four years old, so bad to shoe that it seemed almost impossible to do anything with them.

Youth is the time when so many colts are spoiled for shoeing ever after, for the lesson they learn in the blacksmith shop when they are young they never forget. If they experience kindness they will not show fear. If they meet with abuse, then it is trouble you will get with the most of them afterward. I have seen colts, and even old horses, all right until they got to the shop, and then they were ready for almost anything except what you wanted of them. Don't ever abuse the colt, then you will never have to abuse the horse.

Here is a common incident: John is shoeing a horse, a very lively piece of horse flesh. He goes up to him on the rush, grabs the leg, and tries to get the foot in a position to take the shoe off; but the first thing he knows he is doubled over his box and sprawling on the floor. The next thing he does is to grab a cudgel or his hammer and attempt to beat into that horse the idea that he has done something wrong, but the horse can't see it in that light. He is all ready for fighting now, and every blow John strikes he tries to return, but he is tied in such a manner he cannot make much return. He jumps from one side to the other and thrashes things in general. John thinks he will now do just what he tells him, so he picks up that foot again, but the next thing he knows he is trying to stand on his head on the pile of old shoes. John is very mad now. He is going to make that horse stand anyway, if he works all day. This time he is a little afraid, so he goes up to that horse careful, but the horse doesn't believe in it, and John finds that the horse has got the best of him; he won't be coaxed nor petted; he is mad, too, now, and John gives it up, saying, "He's an ugly beast, and can't be shod." Well, that horse must be shod, but John has got all he wants of the job. Jack comes along and says: "Why don't you rope him, or tie one leg to his jaw?" The horse is roped and tied so he cannot kick or plunge without falling. The horse stands and they shoe him, but it is hard work and takes time and makes men bad-tempered, besides spoiling the horse's disposition.

The next time that horse is shod John isn't around, so George takes hold of him. He tries to kick him, but George won't let him, but steps up to him and pats him, and tries to coax him. The horse says: "No, sir; I am all ready to fight." But George says: "I won't fight." So he sends a boy out for a quart of apples, and takes a couple of them and gives one to the horse.

Well, now, that is a surprise party to that beast. He doesn't think best to give up yet, so George gets some sugar and more apples and gives them to him, and shoes him, not without some trouble, but with nothing like what John experienced. He says the next time he shoes that horse he will stand first-rate, and we think he will.

That man is worth two like John for work. Customers that love their horses like to see them used well, and those are the men who usually pay well for having their horses shod, and no man ought to have a horse who will abuse it himself or allow others to do so in shoeing or any other way.

George was shoeing another horse afterward. He went to work and trimmed his feet carefully where they needed it, and in trimming he found one hind foot broken and torn away, so he couldn't trim it much. Well, he didn't go to work and put on a pair of great heavy shoes which took spikes to hold them there, but he got a nice pair of steel ones which were lighter and yet stiff and wouldn't bend and give way every time the horse started up. Then he fitted them up neatly, and cooled them off when he fitted them to the horse's feet, not hot enough to burn anywhere, but just to mark for his clip-cutting. Then he filed those shoes, the edges especially, so there wouldn't be anything rough to cut his legs with. In punching those shoes he did it very fine and small, so when he got ready to drive them he could drive a very small nail and hold his shoes on until they were worn out. He commenced with the toe-nails and worked back. He didn't work as if he were driving those nails into a block of wood. He seemed to feel that he could hurt that horse if he wasn't careful. When he had them driven on, the horse stepped down on that foot as if he liked the shoe and knew it was put there for his benefit. Then he finished

it up, and in filing under his nails was careful not to weaken
the clinch, but left it just as strong as he could. In hammering the clinches, the nails being small, he didn't have
to do so much pounding to get them bedded. He set those
clinches down with the body of the nail and riveted them,
not simply bending them over and hammering them flat,
because then they would spring and not bed in the horn,
and would work loose and show up in a little while, and
perhaps set the horse to cutting his ankles. Then he filed
them off smooth, and he had a nice small, strong clinch.
He didn't use the file or rasp over the whole of that foot,
but took off the rough horn below the nails, and the place
where he stepped on his foot with a sharp calk, filing very
smooth and thin so as to give the foot a chance to grow
solid and strong and not keep cracking all of the time to
finally end in a seam in the foot half way round his quarters
—a bad foot to put nails into.

Then he got a pair of shoes somewhat wider in the web
for his forward feet and somewhat heavier. Those shoes
were concave, so they would not bear on the sole. He fitted
them light on the heels. He used about one size larger of
nails and drove them carefully as with the hind ones, using
only six nails. He didn't want to tie his foot too tight and
have the nails too far back on the quarter where it was very
meaty. He put two clips on these shoes, too, and quarter
clips which held almost as much as the nails, and kept the
foot solid, and took the greater part of the strain off the
nails.

Great care should be taken to fit shoes level on the feet,
as it is impossible to keep shoes on tight or long unless they
are fitted with a bearing all around the wall except the heels.
A foot may be made to look quite nice by filing it all over
on the outside, but it is not good for the foot.

Where there is an overgrowth of toe and a very thick wall
it is always best to thin it down and weaken it, but it is not

so necessary to do so any farther than up to the hair; it checks the growth of the wall, makes it grow very thin and also very slow.

Too much cannot be said on the failure of horse owners to keep their horses' feet in a growing condition. A foot never grows but perishes when allowed to get dry and hard. Keep the feet as soft as practicable, and you will keep them growing and overcome many difficulties which are not thought of in the general line of horseshoeing.—*By* W. B.

Rules for Horseshoeing.

There is great diversity of opinion existing among smiths with regard to the best method of applying shoes to horses' feet. It is my belief that the best system is that which interferes least with the natural functions, position, and action of the feet. I favor a shoe which affords the most protection to the foot and yet allows the frog to come in contact with the ground.

No specific rule can be obtained in the general art of shoeing, for the simple reason that the feet differ very much under the conditions of health and disease ; hence a certain form of shoe well adapted to meet the requirements of one condition might prove positively injurious in another, as is often the case.

It is generally understood that the hoof is sufficiently elastic to guard against the jar and concussion which occur every time the horse's feet are planted on the ground. This elasticity, as observed in a healthy and unfettered hoof, occurs in downward and backward directions. It is scarcely perceptible, yet wisely is it so ordained, for if there was much expansibility or lateral motion to the hoof it would prove ruinous to the foot, and the chances of securing a shoe to it without positive injury would be very small. Nature has provided this elasticity by leaving the hoof open at the heels, between which is interposed a soft, elastic substance known as the frog.

The parts within the hoof known as the laminæ, or leaves, articulate with each other, and the extent of their articulation corresponds with the contraction and expansion of the hoof, modified, of course, under the influence of partial or complete pressure while traveling. Now, in order to favor this physiological action of the foot the nails must not be inserted any nearer the heels than the safety of the shoe requires; for should the shoe be nailed all around, as the saying is, the hoof, at its solar border, is fettered; hence the action of articulation cannot occur, and the horse soon becomes lame. If possible the frog should be allowed to come in contact with the ground, for it acts as a pad and very much lessens the jar or concussion which otherwise must necessarily occur. The nature of the ground over which the animal travels determines the form, character, and endurance of the frog. Thus in the unshod colt we usually, in a healthy foot, find the frog well formed, prominent, and callous; this is the result of the stimulating hard knocks it receives when traveling. On the other hand, should we examine some horses' feet after they have been long submitted to the evils of domestication (which include faulty shoeing), we shall find that the frog is often imperfect, both in function and structure. I would not have any one infer from these remarks that the blacksmith is always blamable for the loss of the frog, etc., for in the winter, when the roads are a mass of sleet and ice, calks seem to be necessary, and, under such circumstances, it is almost impossible to bring the frog in contact with the ground; hence it may deteriorate.

Then, again, there are various diseases of the foot which interfere with the integrity of the frog as well as that of other parts which enter into the composition of a horse's foot. It is the custom of some shoers to cut away the frog.

There are several reasons why a large portion of the frog should not be removed, and I will briefly allude to some of them. In the healthy frog there is a solid, wedge-like portion of horn, extending from the cleft to the point of the same. It lies directly under that small yet very important bone known as the " navicular," and this bone and its contiguous tissues often become the seat of a very painful disease. This disease often arises in consequence of removing the bulbous prolongation termed the anterior point and bulb of the frog, the function of which is to protect, to a certain extent, this bone and the sensitive parts connected with it from the injuries which might otherwise occur when the animal is made to travel fast over hard and uneven roads. The intelligent shoer is certainly aware that if the frog be cut away, so that nothing but the shoe comes in contact with the earth, the body of the animal has little if any sole support. Hence arises a strain on the laminæ, and finally the descent of the sole.

When preparing the foot in view of applying the shoe, it may be proper to remove just about as much of loose and rough portions of the frog as the animal might wear off provided he were not shod ; and yet, according to the testimony of eminent authorities, this is not always good policy, for these ragged-looking parts usually serve as a protection to new formations beneath, and should not be removed until the latter are perfected.—*By* C. A. S.

Observations on Horseshoeing.

Is it proper that a horse should be shod ? Ought a man to go without shoes because he was born barefooted ? In answer to the first question I would say that the labor that is imposed upon a horse, and the character of the roadway over which he is driven, make it necessary that he should be shod for protection to his hoofs. It is a well-ascertained fact that on pavement, iron shoe and iron toe, calks are preferable, as far as advantage of footing to the horse are concerned. The adhesion of iron toe calks is a material advantage. He is not as liable to slip as when the calks are of steel. I speak of roadways free from ice. The hardened nature of steel deprives it of that property of friction which soft iron has when coming in contact with stone pavements. The slipping of a horse's shoe often strikes sparks upon the pavement. Can such sudden slips be favorable to the horse's limbs when heavily laden ? Steel is used in the light of economy, but can it be said to be very beneficial to the draught horse ?

The shoeing of a horse, as seen by a casual observer, appears to be something or nothing, as the case may be. Let us inquire how the smith operates. He appears to be sharpening something. Having tried the edge of the knife, he is ready to go to work at the horse in waiting. He puts his hand upon the horse and pats him, speaking kindly to him. Kindness to a horse is good common-sense on the part of either owner or smith. He raises the foot and places it between his knees and cuts off seven nails. He appears to be looking for something. Now it is found. It was the eighth nail he was after. To leave it would have been dangerous to the foot, consequently the smith was very eager to find it. The shoe is now loosened at the heels and each nail is removed separately. He makes a fulcrum bearing on the shoe, instead of wrenching it off by main force by putting the pincers under it and prying violently against the sole of the foot. This latter method is very detrimental, especially to a tender-footed horse. The hind shoes are removed, the hoof leveled, and the sole merely cleaned off.

The front shoe is next fitted at a low degree of heat in the iron for the sake of convenience, as the metal is tougher and also more pliable when slightly warm. As this does not burn the hoof, no harm is done. The shoe is clipped in front in order to prevent it from going back. The hoof is cut away in order to let the clip in. Nature has provided for the protection of the front of the hoof by locating a thicker crust at that point. The iron clip affords still additional protection.

A corn is observed at the heel of one of the front feet. Here is the cause of so much uneasiness in the horse. To treat the corn the smith removes the surface as much as required, sometimes to a considerable depth, and pours spirits of salt on it if bare. In some cases blue-stone, pulverized, is used. Some smiths employ tar, tallow and, cotton mixed. Pure pine balsam is a most excellent article for the purpose. Relieving the part of pressure where the corn appears is the principle aimed at in shoeing. The shoe is placed on and the nails are not drawn tight at the side where the corn is.

The peculiarities of horses when brought to be shod are observed by the smith. Holding down a horse's tail sometimes keeps him quiet during the operation. Some require a twitch on the upper lip, while others will not stand it there, so that it is put on the lower lip. The throwing of a bad horse with rings and straps is better than stocking him. A horse when on the ground lies easily, but in the stocks there is a strain that is no ways beneficial to him.

The paring of the hoof requires some thought. Some pare until warned to stop by the sole giving away under the knife. This is a gross error. Remove the dead part of the sole and no more. An examination of the internal structure of the hoof proves most conclusively that the bars are for strength for that part that terminates at the heels. Open the heels well, not sharp at the extreme part of the opening, as if cut with a sharp chisel, but round at the base. Level the crust to that point that experience dictates. Cut down the toe as much as possible, so as to take away that spreading character that the foot will assume when not properly dressed. If the foot is healthy, fit the shoe level at all points. If the horse is tender-footed, leave the shoe off at the heels a little by bending it, but not by cutting the heels away.

Some smiths use a taper piece of iron heated red-hot for burning the hoof at the heels away from the shoe after it is in position. This is a most grievous error, and should not be countenanced at all. Drive the shoe with the strongest nails at the toe and the lightest at the quarter. Cut the clinches with sharp pincers. Remove the broken hoof under the nails slightly, and clinch with the hammer so as not to start the nail back.

Always use a good-sized clinching iron in preference to the large pincers for clinching. Cut off the projecting hoof, if there be any, with a sharp instrument made for that purpose. Finish the hoof in a workmanlike manner, with the rasp below the clinches, to the size of the shoe. Run the corner of the file around the edge of the foot, so as to remove the edge. Do not file the clinches too much, as it reduces their strength. Finish with the fine-cut side of the rasp, or, for fine work, with a fine, hardened file. It is preferable, in all cases, to file as little as possible, but there are instances where the rasp must be used, and in which the non-filing argument is completely set aside.--*By* C. S.

A Country Blacksmith on Shoeing.

Few blacksmiths comprehend what a complicated piece of machinery the foot of a horse is. They do not realize the fact that one careless blow will often stop the working of this machine. Too many smiths when paring the foot cut down the heel and give the toe but little attention. I can only account for this on the theory that the heel is the most convenient part of the foot to work on. This paring of the heel and braces of the foot causes in many instances contracted heels. The heels of a horse should be kept up well and the toe should be kept down. By lowering the heel you thrown the entire weight of the horse on the back tendons of the legs, and thereby produce lameness from over-taxing a very important set of tendons. By keeping up the heel you throw the weight upon the wall of the foot, and in this position stumbling is generally prevented.

I say it is wrong to pare the sole of the foot as some smiths do. Very little, if any, paring should be done to the sole. The braces should not be pared. All or most of the cutting, paring, and smoothing of the frog, brace, bars, or soles is an injury to the horse, making him less valuable to his owner. Nearly all the corns in horses' feet are produced by this process of paring.

The frogs have been placed in the foot by nature to expand the wall of the foot, and as soon as you cut the frog the oily substance begins to leak out. The frog dries up and becomes hard. The wall gets dry and hard and then cracks. I say no man who owns a horse should ever allow a blacksmith to cut the frogs, braces, or soles of his feet. I don't think any smith ever saw a contracted foot which had a good frog. By throwing the weight upon the frogs you force them up between the walls and cause them to spread, and I think the only cure for contracted feet is the method of assisting nature to grow a good frog, which in turn will act as a wedge, crowding out the walls, and soon contraction will be no more.

I don't think it right to use a red-hot shoe in fitting ; it extracts too much moisture from the hoof. I believe the walls of the feet should never be rasped above the clinches, and they should be rasped as little below the clinches as possible. All rasping and filing on the outside of the foot tends to weaken the wall by cutting the fibres of the foot.

As to how a shoe should be put on, I will just say that in all cases you should get the shoe as near the size and shape of the foot as it can be made with the foot and shoe level. Always be careful to get the foot as straight as possible, and if it is not perfectly straight be sure and make the outside a little the lowest. Spread the heels as wide as possible, set the outside a little under, and keep the toes full. Allow me to say also that the foregoing directions will do in most cases, but not in all, there being a few exceptions even to the rules I have given.—*By* H. S.

CHAPTER II.

SPECIAL TOOLS USED BY HORSESHOERS.

The different devices described and illustrated in this chapter have been found useful in many shops and will doubtless prove valuable acquisitions to many others.

Making a Shoeing Hammer.

In making the hammer shown in the accompanying illustrations, I first take a piece of ¾-inch steel, six inches long,

Fig. 5.—Making a Shoeing Hammer by the method of " C. N. S." The Piece of Steel used.

as shown in Fig. 5, which is then " stove up," as shown in Fig. 6, then a ⅜-inch hole is drilled in it and worked out with

Fig. 6.—Showing how the Steel is Shaped.

an eye punch. I next cut out the slit for the claw and then finish with a file. This hammer is better than any that can be bought. Fig. 7 represents it completed.—*By* C. N. S.

Hoof Pincers.

I have a pair of hoof pincers that are very handy. They are made as shown in the accompanying illustration, Fig. 8, one side being blunt so that it can rest against the outside of the hoof, and the other side, being made sharp like a

Fig. 7.—Showing the Shoeing Hammer Completed.

knife, so that it will go past the blunt part as in a pair of scissors. One of the handles is bent over to prevent the fingers being pinched.—*By* H. R.

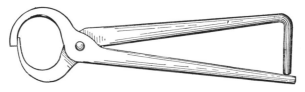

Fig. 8.—A Pair of Hoof Pincers, as made by " H. R."

Making a Pair of Hoof Trimmers.

The accompanying illustration, Fig. 9, represents my method of making a pair of hoof trimmers or pincers.

One pair is made thinner than the other, and is beveled on one side. The piece *A* measures 11 inches from the key to the end of the handle. The end of *B* is turned down so as to prevent the points of the jaws from striking together beyond the desired joint. The jaws are of good cast steel, and are made 1¼ inches wide. The handles are of ½-inch iron.—*By* F. X. Z.

Tool for Clinching Horse Nails.—Rivet Cutter.

I inclose you a draught of two tools made by myself. Fig. 10 is for clinching horseshoe nails, and is a very useful tool for colts or horses who will not stand hammering on their hoofs. I have used it on all horses. The whole length is 14 inches, and it is all made of iron except at *A*, which is made of iron and steel, and has, at *C*, grooves or notches filed in it to pull down the clinch, *B* being under the head

Fig. 9.—A Pair of Hoof Trimmers, as made by " F. X. Z."

of the nail. It should be used in this manner: Prepare the nail the same as if you were going to use the hammer and iron, then take the tongs and pull down the clinch. If necessary, you can use the hammer if any of the clinches should be a little rough. Then rasp as usual. It is difficult to give the exact shape of this tool on paper, but after a blacksmith makes one he will soon learn, by trying it on a few horses, the right shape to give it, and would not then be willing to do without it.

Fig. 11 is a tool for cutting rivets and small bolts, the ends of which project too far. It is all made of steel. Entire length, 16 inches. *A* is the cutting edge; *B* is a short lever running from C to D, which you will easily see gives power enough to cut off the end of a $\frac{5}{16}$-inch rivet. They can be made any size. This also is a very useful tool.—*By* RAB OF THE WYNDE.

Bending Horse Nails. — Spring-Pincers. — A Shoeing Stand.

I have been shoeing horses for thirty years and through

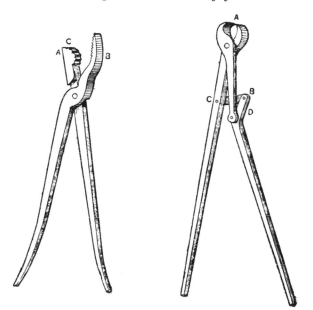

Fig. 10.—Horse Nail Clincher.   Fig. 11.—A Rivet Cutter.

many of these followed the old plan of twisting the nail off with the claw-hammer, which always leaves a rough and dangerous stub. But about ten years ago my hammer broke and being in a hurry I adopted a new plan with such success that I have adhered to it ever since. It is this: As soon as the nail comes through a little, I pull the point over a trifle, then drive the nail up and instead of twisting the end I hit it a light blow, which bends it around in the shape represented in Fig. 12 of the accompanying illustrations, in which the position of the nail is shown before and after bending. This leaves it in a safe position to draw down

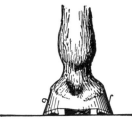

Fig. 12.—Bending Horse Nails by the Method of "P. B. G." The Nail Before and After Bending.

and one not dangerous to man or horse. Since I followed this plan I have never torn my apron or pants or scratched my hands. My customers often wonder why my hands are not scarred like those of other smiths. The pincers I use are shown in Fig. 13. They have a spring in them which

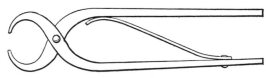

Fig. 13.—The Pincers.

keeps them always open and ready to take hold quickly.

Fig. 14 represents a shoeing stand I use. It is a movable block with a staff that has a block of iron at the top to set the foot on. This stand makes the job of shoeing easier for both man and horse.—*By* P. B. G.

Making a Clincher.

The clincher shown in the accompanying illustrations is one that I have never seen described in any paper. The handles are drawn so as to taper both ways, because that allows them to pass each other easily in drawing down a clinch. The piece B, shown with the fulcrum E in Fig. 15, is fullered so that the nail head can be admitted into the depressions.

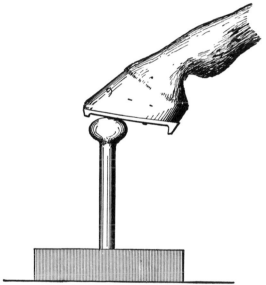

Fig. 14.—The Shoeing Stand.

There must be a small space left between the keyhole in the fulcrum and the jaw, so that B can move up and down. Use for the key the point of a nail that has been nipped off in shoeing, bending it so that it will not come out. If the piece A has the proper curve, any clinch can be caught. In using the tool it should be pulled up, instead of down, as you would the ordinary clinch.

Fig. 15 is a top view of the piece *B*, Fig. 16 is a top view of *C*, Fig. 17 is a top view of *A*, and Fig. 18 shows the clincher completed.—*By* A. H. H.

Fig. 15.—Making a Clincher by the Method of "A. H. H." Top View of the Piece *B*

Shoeing Box.

I send herewith a sketch, Fig. 19, of my shoeing box. The

Fig. 16.—Top View of the Piece *C*.

dimensions are as follows: The height at the back is 10 inches; the length is 18 inches; the height of the front is 6

Fig. 17.—Top View of the Piece *A*.

inches; the feet are 7 inches; the width is 10 inches. The feet extend the full depth of the box, and the sides and ends

Fig. 18.—The Clincher Completed.

are fastened to them by screws. The bail is of half-inch iron, fastened by two bolts at each side. A flat piece of iron is nailed around the top to protect the edges of the wood. I lay the rasp behind the bail. I like this pattern better than any I have ever seen.—*By* BILLY BLACKSMITH.

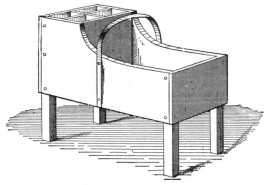

Fig. 19.—Horseshoer's Tool Box.

Horseshoer's Tool Box.

The inclosed sketches will, I think, make the construction and proportions of two handy shoeing boxes intelligible. The

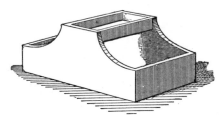

Fig. 20.—One Style of Horseshoer's Tool Box.

boxes are carried by the hand placed under the till at the top. The box shown in Fig. 20 is what may be called a double box, while that of Fig. 21 might be termed a single

box. Both styles are in request among shoers, some pre-
ferring one and some the other.—*By* K. W. G.

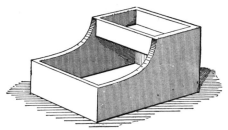

Fig. 21.—Another Style of Horseshoer's Tool Box.

Tool Box.

The inclosed sketches represent a tool box which I have
used for the past twenty years. I find it very convenient

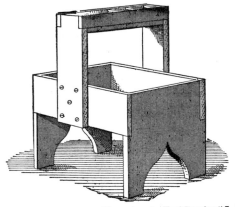

Fig. 22.—Perspective View of Horseshoer's Tool Box by "L. H."

to have the tool receptacle raised from the floor, because it
brings the tools so much nearer the place where they are
wanted. Fig. 22 is a perspective view. The dimensions indi-

cated upon the drawings, Figs. 23 and 24, show the proportions I have found most desirable for employment. The till at the top of the " deck " is made one inch deep. The tool box is made four inches deep. From this brief description and the accompanying sketches I think any one will be able to construct such a tool box as we countrymen use. —*By* L. H.

Shoeing Box.

I send inclosed a sketch of a shoeing box, Fig. 25, which has many advantages. The dimensions are as follows:

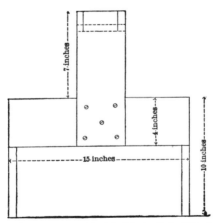

Fig. 23.—Side Elevation of " L. H.'s" Tool Box. Scale 1½ inches to the foot.

Length, 12 inches ; width, 18 inches, and height 10 inches. The small square compartments are for nails, the larger space in front of them is for knives, while the other half of the upper portion of the box contains rasps, hammers, pincers, etc. The drawer below, which in the sketch is shown partly drawn out, is quite convenient in cases where the smith is obliged to go away from his shop to work, as, for instance, to attend to a lame or sick horse. Part of the drawer is used for extra sharp knives, and such tools as are required upon special occasions, while the other half is used for bottles of acids, can of tar, rosin, etc. When the drawer is closed it is held in place by the latch shown in the sketch. The feet and strap work on the sides of the box are of iron. The handle by which the box is moved is of

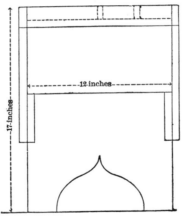

Fig. 24.—End Elevation of " L. H.'s" Tool Box. Scale 1½ inches to foot.

wood, and is fastened between the irons by two long screws. A ferrule is put upon each end of the wooden handle in order to prevent its splitting.—*By* NOW AND THEN.

An Improved Farrier's Box.

The bottom of a farrier's box should slope up as shown in Figs. 26 or 27 in the accompanying illustrations. Then tools are within sight and reach, and one is not obliged to stoop low nor to feel around for them. Boxes are made too large. One wants but few tools in them, and these should stick out handy to be seen and seized. A square bottom causes the accumulation of parings and old nails. With sloping sides these can be brushed out without emptying the nail boxes above.—*By* WILL TOD.

An Improved Rest for a Horse's Foot.

The accompanying illustration, Fig. 28, represents a device for a horse's foot to rest on while the smith draws down the

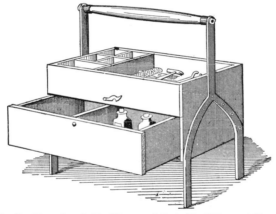

Fig. 25.—Horseshoer's Tool Box, contributed by " Now and Then."

clinches. It is easily made and is a great improvement on the old style of foot rests with three legs. To make this new rest take first a piece of hardwood plank 28 inches long and 12 inches wide. Make a 2x4 inch hole, three inches from the end of the plank, and place in it the upright piece, 2x4 inches and 18 inches long, as shown in the illustration. Make the top of this piece a little rounding, and run an iron brace from the plank to the piece. Make four pins from ⅜-inch round iron and drive one of them in each corner of the

plank, letting them extend out half an inch.   These answer
as legs and prevent the rest from sliding.

To use the rest put it far enough ahead of the horse to
make his knee almost straight.   The smith stands with one
foot on the plank and draws the clinches on the off side of
the foot.   When the clinches are finished on that side, the
smith turns to the other side of the foot and completes the

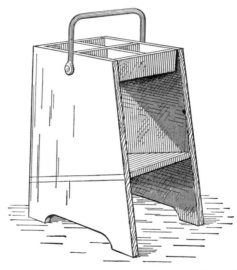

Fig. 26.—Showing Arrangement of the Bottom of Farrier's Box.

job.   If the horse moves to get his foot away from the rest
he must tip it over the long end, and he cannot do this because the smith is standing on this end.   The pins prevent
his sliding the rest along the floor, and the position of his
foot on the rest is such that he cannot lift it easily, and if
you bear down his knee, so as to make it remain straight, he
cannot raise his foot at all.—*By* E. K. W.

Making a Shoeing Stand.

I will try to describe a shoeing stand, made of wood, which is superior to anything I have ever seen. It will save a smith a great many bruises. Fig. 29, of the accompanying illustrations, represents the post with a tenon on the bottom 2x2x2 inches. The post at the shoulder is 3x3 inches and at the top is $2\frac{1}{4}$x$2\frac{1}{4}$ inches and 17 inches long. The corners may be champfered or not, as thought best. Fig. 30 represents the base, which is 16 inches in

Fig. 27.—Showing another Form for the Bottom of Farrier's Box.

diameter, with a mortise in the center 2x2 inches, and four grooves in it to receive the braces. The four braces, represented by one shown in Fig. 31, are made of $1\frac{1}{4}$x$\frac{5}{16}$-inch iron bent almost at right angles. Fig. 32 represents the stand completed. It requires one dozen $\frac{5}{16}$-inch bolts to make it strong, four being $3\frac{3}{4}$x$\frac{5}{16}$ inches each, and eight $2\frac{1}{4}$x$\frac{5}{16}$ inches each.

The woodwork should be made from good seasoned oak or other hardwood. The base is made as shown, in order that a man can stand on it with both feet. The base is 2 inches thick by 16 inches in diameter and is grooved to receive the brace irons.—*By* C. E. V.

A Handy Shoeing Stand.

I give herewith a drawing, Fig. 33, of a handy shoeing

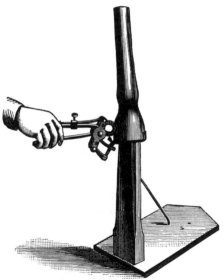

Fig. 28.—Improved Foot Rest, made by " E. K. W."

stand. It is made of three pieces of ⅜-inch square, 2 feet long, and spread so that the legs will form an equilateral triangle, and be about 16 inches high. The more spread the more stable it is. When the horse moves, this stand can be kicked about and moved along accordingly. It is used for the fore feet only.—*By* A. H. H,

A Tool for Drawing Clips and Sharpening Toe Calks.

I will endeavor, with the aid of the accompanying engravings, to give your readers an accurate idea of a tool I use for sharpening toe calks and drawing clips on shoes. In making the tool I first take a piece of 1½-inch square steel about 8 inches long, and draw it out on one end, so that for about 3 inches it will fit in the square hole of the anvil. I

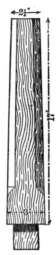

Fig. 29 shows the Post of the Shoeing Stand.

then hammer it down in the anvil until it is a solid fit, and then heat it again put it in the anvil hole and by hammering against it bend it square, turning it to the side of the anvil opposite that where I stand. I next take my cutter and cut it down, beginning three-quarters of an inch from the side of the anvil, so as to leave a stem about ⅝-inch square coming out from the center of the bottom of the tool. This stem is to support the shoe while drawing on the clip. I then take a half round cutter and cut out a slot at the corner of the tool so that the clip can go easily in it, and the tool is completed. In using it for drawing clips I weld

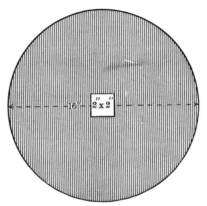

Fig. 30.—The Base of the Shoeing Stand.

the toe to the shoe, then hold the shoe out on the end of the tool, allowing it to rest on the stem, and draw the clip to-

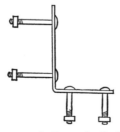

Fig. 31.—Showing how the Braces for the Stand are made.

ward me. With this tool I can draw three good clips in the time it usually takes to draw one from the corner of the anvil. When the clip is on I stand the shoe endwise on the anvil, allowing the clip to hide in the slot. The shoe being backed by the tool I place my fuller on the toe and draw it down. By following the method I have just described you will find it the neatest and easiest way of clipping or sharpening. Fig. 34 represents the tool; *A* indicates the stem, and *B* is the slot. *C* is the part made to fit the anvil. Fig. 35 shows the method of drawing clips. Fig. 36 illus-

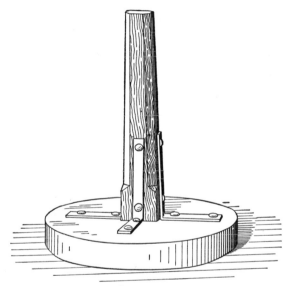

Fig. 32 —Showing the Shoeing Stand Completed.

trates how the shoe should be placed when the calks are to be sharpened.—*By* J. J. C.

Sharpening Calks.

I will describe my plan for sharpening horseshoes :

I first take an old axle two inches square, cut it in two in the center, and then upset one of the pieces at the end where it was cut off, so that it is about 3 inches by 1¾ inches on the end. Then I lay a piece of horseshoe rasp on the end, as shown at *A* in Fig. 37 of the accompanying engravings, and

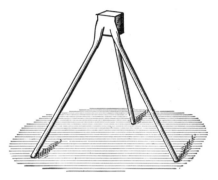

Fig. 33.—A Shoeing Stand, made by "A. H. H."

after drawing it to the required shape, as shown at *A*, Figs. 37 and 38, I bend the piece, as shown in Fig. 37 at *B*, punch a ⅝-inch hole through it at *C* and *D*, heat the end where the

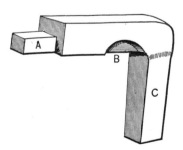

Fig. 34.—Side View of the Tool used for Drawing Clips and Sharpening Toe Calks.

steel was laid on and harden it so that it will not fly when struck with the hammer, which completes this part of the job.

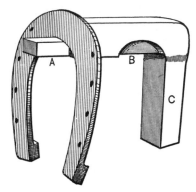

Fig. 35.—Showing the Method of Drawing Clips.

I then take a piece of iron 1½ inches square and about 3 feet long, jump a piece of the same size across the end of it as

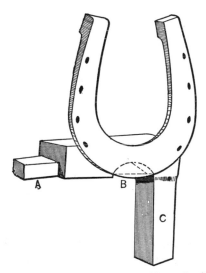

Fig. 36.—Showing the Tool as Used for Sharpening Calks.

shown at *S*, Fig. 39, and upset it to the same length as the width of Fig. 38 at *A*, which is three inches or any width you wish to make it. I then bend it into shape as shown at *E*, Fig. 37, and weld a piece of iron at *F*, making two lugs in the ends of which I punch two ⅝-inch holes; I fit the lugs to the first piece so that the two holes correspond with the hole *C*, then I let the bottom end extend to the ground, as shown

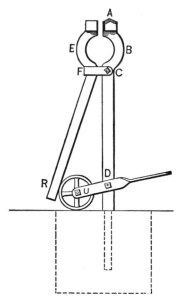

Fig. 37.—Machine for Sharpening Calks.

at *R*, Fig. 37. I next provide myself with a cast-iron wheel six inches in diameter by two across the face, and taking a piece of iron about four feet long, 2x⅜ inch, bend it edge-ways as shown at Fig. 40, and twist the ends as shown in Fig. 41, leaving them wide enough apart to go each side of the wheel. I then drill a hole in each end as shown at *I*,

Fig. 41, and two at K, Fig. 41, being careful to place the holes at K far enough from the wheel to make that end heavy enough to fall at all times. I then put one end on each side of Fig. 40 insert the bolt as shown at D, Fig. 39, and put a bolt through the wheel and the ends as shown at Fig. 37. I next take a block of wood about two feet long and one foot

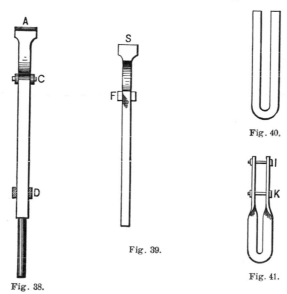

Fig. 38.

Fig. 39.

Fig. 40.

Fig. 41.

Fig. 38.—Side View of One of the Parts. Fig. 39.—Side View of the Opposite Part. Fig. 40.—Showing the Piece Bent for Attachment to the Wheel. Fig. 41.—Showing the Piece ready for Attachment to the Wheel and to the Piece shown in Fig 39.

in diameter, and bore a hole in one end of it large enough to let the axle end into it and drive it into the block as tightly as possible. I then dig a hole in the floor of the shop, put the block into it and fill it up as solid as possible, which completes the job. This arrangement enables me to sharpen toes and calkings in half the time required to do it on the anvil. It is also handy as a vise for bending iron in, as it is always ready; all you have to do is to put your iron or shoe in the machine and your foot on the lever, and your work is fast until you take your foot off, when the

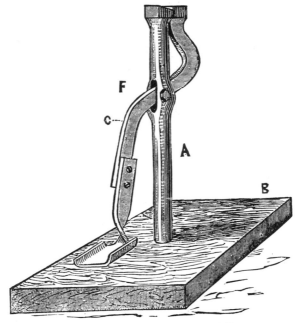

Fig. 42.—A Tool for sharpening Toe Calks.

wheel drops and the jaws open, releasing the work immediately.—*By* A. S.

A Tool for Sharpening Toe Calks.

I send a sketch, Fig. 42, of a handy tool for sharpening toe calks.

A represents a piece of round shafting with steel face at top. *B* represents a block of wood, into which the shaft *A* is let. *C* passes through *A*, at the slot *F*. The foot piece

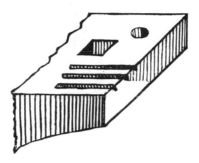

Fig. 43.—Device to Prevent Horseshoes from Slipping on the Anvil.

is bolted or riveted to *C*. The steel face is $3\frac{1}{2}$ inches wide and slanted, as shown in the drawing.—*By* WILL.

A Device to Prevent Horsehoes Slipping on the Anvil.

The following is a good plan to prevent horseshoes from slipping on the anvil. I have been bothered in this way for years, but last winter I took an old anvil and cut three creases in it near the hardy hole, as shown in the engraving, Fig. 43. This ended all my trouble. It works like a charm.—*By* S. C. R.

Getting the Angle for a Horse's Foot.

The accompanying illustration, Fig. 44, represents the tool I use in getting the angle of a horse's foot. The bar or pointer is eight inches long, and one-eighth inch thick. A small thumbscrew secures it to the other piece, which is made from iron one inch wide and one-quarter inch thick. In making it I take a piece twelve inches long, and then another piece, bending the latter into a half circle as in the

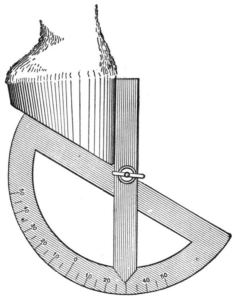

Fig. 44.—Tool used by " A. W. M." for getting the Angle of a Horse's Foot.

illustration, and then welding together the four ends of the two pieces. The method of using the tool is clearly shown in the illustration.—*By* A. W. M.

CHAPTER III.

VARIOUS DEVICES FOR SHOEING UGLY HORSES.

Such a variety of plans for shoeing unruly horses and mules with the least possible risk to the shoer, is presented herewith, that a selection may be made, probably, to fit almost all cases.

Shoeing Vicious Horses.

I will give my way of handling bad kicking horses in shoeing. When I get a horse supposed to be vicious I approach him as quietly as possible and notice the eyes and the ears, which show as plainly as words, whether he is really vicious or only nervous. If vicious, I give him a taste of the war bridle, and if that does not work then I give him some rope along with the bridle, which is sufficient in all cases I ever met yet. I use Prof. Rockwell's war bridle sometimes and sometimes Prof. Magner's rope bridle, Fig. 45; either will answer. The rope I use is a $\frac{3}{4}$-inch one, from 21 to 24 feet long. I take a piece of good harness leather, $1\frac{1}{4}$-inch wide and 9 inches long, take two $\frac{5}{16}$-inch rings and some copper rivets, and fasten the rings to each end of the strap. I then tie a loop in one end of the rope so that it will not slip, and put it around the neck. I put the other end of the rope through one ring, then pass the strap around the pastern and the rope through the other ring, then forward through the loop on the neck, pull the foot forward, and I have him—for the hind foot. The front foot

he is apt to use in rearing and plunging, so I strap the foot
up to his arm and then let him plunge till he is ready to
stand.   Then I am ready to go to shoeing.   If he is only
nervous I approach him quietly and coolly ; never under
any circumstances, when I am excited or nervous, as the
horse knows as soon as you approach him whether you are
excited or not.   Do not talk crossly to him.   It is better to
whistle than to scold him.

Always be cool, quiet, and firm, never getting angry.
Control yourself and you can control the horse.   I have

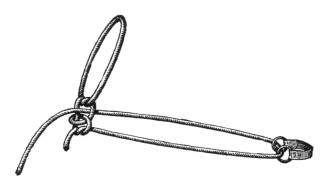

Fig. 45—Showing the Device of " J. C. L." for Shoeing a Kicking Horse.

never had any occasion to use stocks, and in fact never saw
a horse in them.

I have been a practical shoer for twenty-three years and
have shod some of the worst horses in this section of the
country, but have never failed to shoe one that was brought
to me, and they have brought them from quite a distance,
sometimes from as much as ten miles, passing two or three
other shops on the way.—*By* J. C. L.

[Note.—In the accompanying illustration our artist has
drawn the knot loosely so as to show exactly how it is tied.

Of course in practical use the lower knot is to be drawn up tight. The proportions in this illustration have been exaggerated a little so as to make the loops and knots clearer to the reader.—ED.]

How to Shoe Kicking Horses and Mules.

I have shod many kicking horses in the following way: The horse must have a switch tail—the longer the better—to carry out my plan. I place a stick about a foot long in the tail, close to the end of the dock, at B in the illustration, Fig. 46, double back the hair upon it, and confine it

Fig. 46.—" A. C.'s " Method of Shoeing Kicking Horses.

with a piece of twine. Then take a long rope and tie it to the stick in the tail, winding it round and round till it is firm. Then buckle a strap with a ring in it round the ankle, just under the fetlock at A. Let your assistant pass the end of the rope through the ring, and, after going to a respectable distance, pull up the foot as is shown in the sketch. The horse cannot hurt himself. If he throws himself, slacken up the rope till he gets up, and immediately draw his foot up again. He cannot hurt the shoer or lie on him. Some one may say, How will you get the rope on the tail or the strap round the ankle? I have always contrived some way to do it, generally by holding up one of the fore feet. I once shod a horse in this way, that had been all round the county to be shod, and it had been given up as impossible to do in any other way except to cast him. He did not hinder my man more than fifteen minutes, and he always shod well afterwards.—*By* A. C.

[As it would be impossible to shoe a kicking horse having a short tail by the method described by "A. C.," the following is suggested:

With a long rope form a sort of collar, as at *A* in the en-

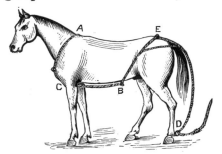

Fig. 47.—Another Plan for Shoeing Kicking Horses.

graving, Fig. 47, then let the rope pass between the fore legs at *C*, and stopping at *B*, pass over and around the body, and tie at *B*. Join another rope at *E*, with braces on each rump, as shown in the illustration. A similar strap to the one used by "A. C." could be buckled around the ankle at *D*, and the rope leading from *E*, passed through the ring in the same manner as suggested by "A. C." Afterwards proceed as "A. C." has described above.—Ed.]

To Shoe Unruly Horses and Mules.

I give, for the benefit of others, my plan of shoeing wild horses, after nearly eighteen years' experience on the Pacific Coast. We employ various methods, but the one I am about to describe answers the purpose very well.

To shoe an unruly horse, take a leather strap three feet long, made like a hame strap, with a loop on the inside; pass it around the fetlock; put the end of the strap through the loop and draw it up close around the fetlock, as shown in the sketch, Fig. 48, at 1. Take up the foot by the strap and buckle the strap around the fore-arm, as at 2. The horse is now compelled to stand on three legs. Drive on the

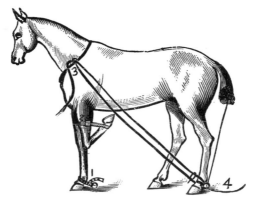

Fig. 48.—Plan for Controlling Vicious Horses.

shoe and clinch it in this position, unless by this process he has become gentle enough to allow you to unbuckle the strap and take his foot and clinch it up in front. When done change the strap to the other side and shoe the other foot. To shoe the hind foot, take a rope (your own judgment will suggest the length and thickness), tie a knot on the end and another knot far enough from the end to pass around his neck. Pass the knot on the end through the other knot and tighten up the latter so that the end knot

cannot slip out. Take the other end of the rope and go
behind your horse and make him step over the rope with
his hind foot. Carry the rope around to his neck and pass
the end through the rope at 3 ; draw up his foot by the
rope till it nearly leaves the ground ; fasten it by taking a
half hitch around both the ropes at 3. Now tie a string
around both ropes, to keep them together, and slide it down
close to his fetlock. Next fasten a ring on a hame strap

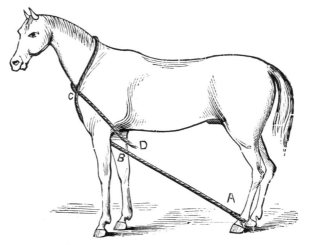

Fig. 49.—Device for Shoeing Ugly Horses.

and buckle the strap around the fetlock, under the rope ;
tie a rope in the tail, pass it through the ring alluded to,
and pull on the rope at 4. This will raise his foot in a position to shoe it without danger to either the horse or the
smith, as the man who holds the rope can set down the foot
and take it up at pleasure. When the shoe is driven on,
either clinch it pulled back or loosen the rope at the neck
and draw it up till the foot comes in a position to clinch it

in the usual way. The horse can't kick you. A little practice will enable the shoer to shoe bad horses or mules without danger.—*By* OLD ROPER.

How to Shoe Kicking Horses and Mules.

I have always found the following to be a safe and easy way to shoe unruly horses or mules. Take a rope 1¼ inches thick, and splice a loop on one end of it large enough to allow the other end of the rope to pass through and work

Fig. 50.—Shoeing a Kicking Mule.

in it with ease. When you have a kicking horse to shoe, lay this rope on the floor, and open out the noose so as to take in the foot which you want to shoe. Then draw the noose up tight around the fetlock at *A*, as shown in the accompanying illustration, Fig. 49. Pass the rope between the fore legs at *B*, and up and over the neck at *C*. Now let some man who will not drop the rope every time the horse moves, hold it at the end *D*, and if the shoer gets hurt it will be his own fault, for there is no necessity of holding the foot more than to keep it steady after it is drawn up from the floor with the rope. This is my plan, but there may be other better ones. In shoeing the fore feet, the shoer must hold and manage the animal the best way he knows how.—*By* SOUTHERN YANKEE.

Shoeing a Kicking Horse or Mule.

I have had considerable experience in shoeing kicking mules and horses, and accordingly inclose a sketch, Fig. 50, to illustrate my method in such cases. I take two pieces of spring steel $1\frac{3}{4}$ inches wide, and long enough to make a good-sized pair of hames, bend them to fit a collar and punch holes in the top to let a strap pass through to fit different sizes of collars. I then take a piece of $1\frac{1}{2}$-inch iron or steel, 6 inches long, rivet it on the flat side of the hame, bend in a circle to clear the collar, and shut a **D** ring in the ends, one on each hame—as shown in the engraving annexed. Tie in the ring a strong $\frac{3}{4}$-inch rope on the side opposite to where you are to work; pass this rope around the fetlock to the other ring, and tie to suit yourself. Hook an open link on the ropes so the animal cannot get his other foot through them, and you have him. When you raise the foot to drive, the rope will be tightened, and he cannot kick you either in driving or clinching.—*By* W. W. K.

Device for Shoeing Vicious Horses.

I will describe my patented device for shoeing vicious horses, as shown in the accompanying illustration, Fig. 51. The sheave net under the tail has a latching wedge which clutches the rope at any place where it is desired to do so. The leg can be taken backward or forward at the will of the shoer, and the horse is held securely, for no amount of struggling and kicking can enable him to get his foot down.

The forelegs are held by a strap and snap which snaps into a ring on the foot. The hindfoot is raised by standing behind the horse and pulling the rope. The wedge is controlled by a small rope running parallel with the other and attached to the wedge.—*By* A. F. TRASK.

Shoeing a Kicking Horse.

In managing kicking horses I use a rope about twenty

Fig. 51.—Device of A. F. Trask for Shoeing Kicking Horses.

feet long and three-quarters of an inch in diameter, and having at one end a loop which I put around the horses' neck like a collar but loosely. Holding the other end I get behind him, let him step over it, then bring the end up to the loop and take a turn or two around it so that it will slip easily, and I can then draw the hind leg off the ground as shown in Fig. 52. When I begin to handle his foot I draw the rope quite tightly and if he plunges around too much I let it down a little.

I have followed this plan for thirty years, have never failed to succeed in shoeing a horse, and have never received a scratch in doing the job.—*By* J. B. G.

Shoeing a Vicious Horse.

The accompanying engraving, Fig. 53, represents a very good method of shoeing a vicious horse. If followed the plan will enable the smith to shoe any horse without putting him in the stocks. The method is as follows:

Fig. 52.—Shoeing a Kicking Horse.

Get a leather strap, two inches wide and four feet in length, with a good buckle on one end. Try it first on a gentle horse. The cut shows how it is put around the fetlock. Put the strap around the fetlock before raising his foot. You then raise his foot, and have some one draw the strap through the buckle as far as possible. Now buckle it and let his foot down. You must repeat this operation on a gentle horse until you know just how it is used. Be sure you have the strap the right way around the fetlock before raising his foot.

When you come to try it on a vicious horse, first take off the harness, and put a rope around his neck in such a way

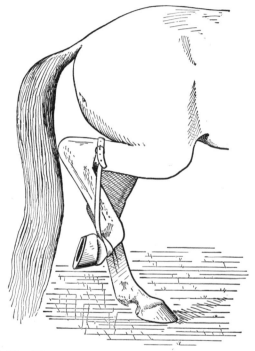

Fig. 53.—Shoeing a Vicious Horse by the Method of "E. K. W."

that it will not choke him. Talk kindly to him, and avoid all excitement around the shop. Rub and pat his hind legs down to his feet. Try and raise his foot, but don't hold him, let him down. Repeat the same until he allows you to keep his foot up a few minutes. Always shoe a bad horse

first on his hind feet. Now put the strap around his fetlock. Be very careful not to get him excited. Put the end
through the buckle before raising his foot. Now you gently raise his foot up, and have your man at the same time
draw the strap through the buckle as tightly as possible.
Now buckle it and put the end of the strap under the leather
loop. Now let him down—don't be uneasy about him get
ting hurt. Let him fight until he will let you handle his
foot. Now put the shoe on and complete the job before letting his foot down. If he will not allow you handle his feet,
walk him around in the shop on three legs. He will get so
tired that he will stand better than any gentle horse will.
On the other foot you will not have so much trouble, and
after you get used to it you can put the strap on alone in
two minutes. Use it only on bad horses and on those that
try to jerk away from you, for it will not hurt them, and it
will not take so much time to do the job. And best of all,
you will not endanger your life by being jerked all over the
shop.—*By* E. K. W.

Stocks or Swings for Shoeing Kicking Horses and Mules.

We have a swing which we made for shoeing kicking
mules and horses, and it works to perfection. It can be
kept in any shop, and when not wanted will not be in the
way. We keep ours over the shoeing floor. The swing has
no frame against which a horse might strike and be bruised.
The cost of this swing is not more than ten or twelve dollars.
The belts or aprons are made of heavy canvas, and it is
better to double the canvas.

Fig. 54, of the accompanying engravings, represents the
breast belt, *A*. It is 10 inches wide and 4 feet long, with a
ring fastening each end, the chain in each ring being 12
inches long. On one side of this belt, about four inches

from the center, is riveted a strap 1½ inch wide and 3 feet long, and about four inches from it on the same side there is riveted a buckle large enough to receive the strap. This strap goes around the neck of the horse like a collar. On the other side of the belt and in the center another buckle

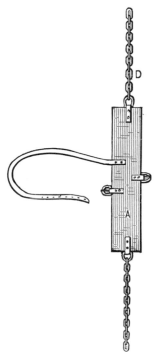

Fig. 54.—A Swing for Shoeing Kicking Horses. The Breast Belt.

is riveted, which is large enough to receive a strap 2 inches wide. The belt B, shown in Fig. 55, is 22 inches wide and 4 feet long, and the four chains riveted to each corner are 12 inches long. Two straps are riveted on this belt in the center, one on each side. The straps are each 2 inches wide and 18 inches long. One of them goes between the front legs and buckles in a buckle on belt *A*, and the other goes between the hind legs and buckles on belt *C*, shown in Fig. 56. This belt is 6 inches wide and 4 feet long, and has rings and chains like those on belt *A*. It has also a buckle in the center.

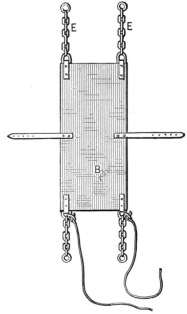

Fig. 55.—The Belly Belt.

In Fig. 57 the swing is shown in position on a horse. *L* in the engraving denotes a pulley wheel about 4 feet in diameter, with a groove in it large enough to allow a ⅜-inch rope to be wound around it five or six times. *K* is a shaft about 6 inches in diameter and 5 feet long. The wheel *L* is fastened to this shaft with a gudgeon of 1⅛-inch iron. *H, H,*

are ¾-inch ropes which pass around the shaft. The length
of these ropes depends upon the height of the smith's shop.
G, G, G, G, are four rings, to which are attached eight
small and very short hooks. These rings are to be fastened
to the ropes H, H. M is the rope which turns the wheel L.

Fig. 56.--The Buttock Belt.

This rope should have a guide so that it will not run off the
wheel.

The belt B has also two small ⅜-inch ropes attached to it.

To use the swing, first blindfold your horse, then tie him
so he cannot break loose. Next lay the belt B on the back

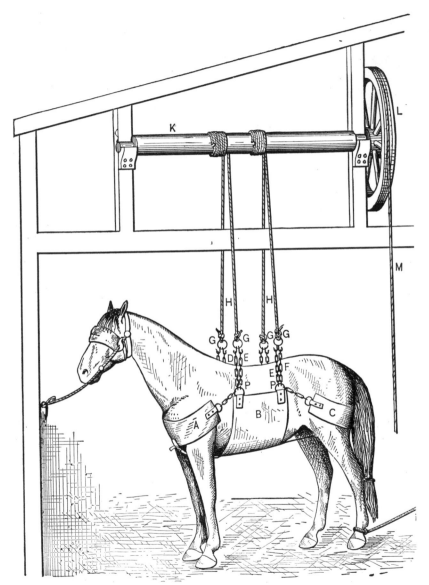

Fig. 57—Showing the Swing in Position and Ready for Use.

of the horse, pass the small ropes on this belt under the horse and fasten them to the rings on the other end of the belt, tying them so that they will allow the belt to slip around to the place shown in the engraving. Then put on the belt A, buckling one strap between the fore legs, adjusting the chains as shown in the illustration. Sometimes another strap is attached to this belt and then passed around the animal's neck. The chains on belt A pass through the front rings on belt B. Belt C is placed on the animal as shown. One end of this belt is tied with a small rope to the back ring in belt B. On the other side of C have a rope about 8 feet long and draw this rope through the back ring in belt B, and then slip the belt down. This rope should be long enough to prevent the horse from kicking you. When he tries to kick it must be pulled tight. The next thing to do is to pass the chains through the back rings on belt A, but you need not hook the chains on belt B to the hooks on G, G, unless the horse is a very large one. If possible buckle the strap behind the hind legs before swinging the horse.

In shoeing the front feet I use a knee strap. In working on the hind feet I tie a rope to the tail and buckle a strap around the fetlock. This trap has a ring through which I pass the rope N. Your man can hold this rope, or you can tie it to anything that is convenient. With this rope you can hold the foot so that you can work on it with ease. Sometimes I put one end of a rope around the fetlock of the other hind leg, bring the other end of the rope up around the neck and tie it. This will prevent kicking. It will raise 2,000 pounds if well built.—*By* D. & K.

Stocks for Kicking Horses.

My method of making stocks for shoeing kicking horses is illustrated in the accompanying engraving, Fig. 58, in

which *B B* represents the sills, 8x8 inches and 10 feet long;
A A are the ties, 4x4 inches and 10 feet long; *C C C C* are the
posts, 6x6 inches and 9 feet long. The crossties connecting
C C C C are 4x6 inches and 3 feet long. The platform *E* fits
loosely in the frame. *F F* are the belts on which the horse
is hung; *G G* are cranks by which the platform is raised
and lowered; *H H* are ropes which connect the roller and
the platform. The frame is made of solid wood. One of
the cranks is fastened solidly and the other is made so that

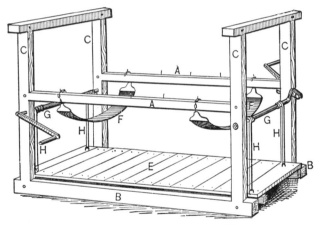

Fig. 58.—Stocks for Shoeing Kicking Horses.

I can take it out to let the horse in. When I get the horse
in I tie him with two straps so that he cannot move his
head from one side to the other. I then raise the platform,
carrying him with it, of course, as high as I desire; the
straps *F* are then hooked over the pins shown in the engravings. These pins are placed to suit any convenience.
I take two belts, put a ring in each end of each belt, and
add four or five links to the end as indicated in the engraving, and when the horse is high enough, I hook the links of

the pins and let the platform drop. The horse can then be shod
with ease. In this way I have shod horses that could not
be handled by any other plan. To make the belts I take
two, each eight inches wide, which makes the belt 16 inches
wide, and it is to be remembered that the wider the belt is
the better.—*By* N. P. S.

Stocks for Shoeing Ugly Mules and Horses.

This stock consists of light wood posts put well down in
the ground. These posts are 12 feet long, 8 feet high, and

Fig. 59.--Stock for Shoeing Ugly Mules.

are set about $2\frac{1}{2}$ feet apart and secured by plates at top, as
shown in illustration, Fig. 59. To the cross piece, 1, is attached the belly-piece, or band, 5. No. 2 is the roller, to
which is attached the belly-band. Nos. 3 and 4 are the levers
for winding up the roller. When wound to the required
height it is held in place by permitting one end of the lever
to strike against the plate, as shown. Two holes should be

mortised through the roller, at right angles to each other, for the accommodation of the levers. Nos. 6 and 7 are movable pieces, which are only in use while the mule or horse is being secured. Then they are detached and laid aside, to give the workman free access to the feet of the animal. At No. 8 two ropes are represented which hold the hind feet while the shoes are being fitted and nailed to the forefoot. If not fastened back the animal is apt to strike forward with his hind feet in his desperate efforts to free himself, and perhaps endanger the shoer. At No. 9 is shown a rope which encircles the neck and is made fast to a cross-piece, as shown in the cut, and its object is to keep the animal from rearing up. No. 10 is a breast strap which keeps the animal from jumping forward. No. 11 is a rope which goes over a roller and down to another roller, to which it is made fast. This latter roller is provided with a crank by which your mule can be drawn into the stocks if he objects to going. This rope serves to hold his head up out of the way, and defeat any sinister purpose the animal may have of using his teeth on the shoer. When I get them into this stock they are safe. I can shoe the worst mule or horse that can be produced in perfect safety. I have been engaged in shoeing horses and mules for 25 years, and have never failed to shoe anything that came to me. Of late, however, I don't fancy being jerked about by ugly mules. In my young days I didn't want any better fun than to get hold of a wild horse or mule.—*By* T. J. PALIN.

CHAPTER IV.

PREPARING THE FOOT. HOT OR COLD FITTING, WHICH?

The advocates of each system of fitting are numerous, but the weight of evidence seems to be in favor of cold fitting, in theory, and more or less hot, in practice. The writer has seen shoers who were, so to speak, warm defenders of the cold method, employ in actual practice, heat enough to mark the surface of the foot so as to indicate where the high spots were. They would permit the shoe to touch the foot only for an instant and the heat in the iron would only be sufficient to slightly discolor the hoof.

Preparing the Horse's Foot for the Shoe.

I desire to make a few remarks on the proper methods of preparing the horse's foot for the shoe. I have had considerable experience—fifteen years as farrier-major in the British Army, and about thirty years in New York City and State—and should, therefore, know whereof I speak.

There are many who think differently from me on the points I shall touch upon, but my long and varied experience has proven my views to be correct—to my own satisfaction.

In the first place, a horseshoer must understand a little of the anatomy of the horse's foot; he must understand the position and composition of those parts of the foot with

which he has to deal; he must know how far the sensitive
membrane of the frog and sole extends, so as to be able to
judge when and where to cut, and where to drive the nails
in adjusting the shoe. It is not necessary that he should
have a thorough scientific knowledge, but just enough to enable him to understand the "art of horseshoeing." It is
for want of even a little of this knowledge that so many
horses are crippled and rendered useless.

A great many horseshoers think nothing of these points,

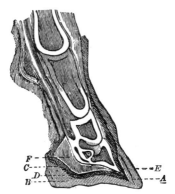

Fig. 60.—Sectional View of the Foot.

but undertake to shoe horses imagining that they have
only a hard block of horn to cut at, burn away and destroy
without inflicting any injury to the foot, and that nothing is
necessary but to make the foot look as "fanciful" as possible (to the great injury of the foot)—anyway, as long as
the horse is shod and no fault found.

Now, this we know (or, at least, ought to know), is not
right. We cannot shoe properly unless we have at least a
little knowledge of the nature of the foot.

I introduce here a cut, Fig. 60, showing a sectional view
of the foot in its natural condition; *A* is the wall of the

hoof, B is the horny frog, C is the sensitive membrane of the frog, D is the sensitive membrane of the sole, E is the sensitive laminæ, and F is the plantar cushion (or sensitive frog).

It can been seen by a glance at the cut where so many mistakes are made in shoeing horses, either by driving a nail into the part marked E, when it becomes inflamed and causes great pain, and will often cause the horse to go lame, or by cutting away at the frog until they strike the sensitive part marked F, when the frog will soon waste away and smell bad, causing navicular disease.

Now, my idea of preparing a foot for a shoe is not to cut away the sole ; merely leveling it off with the rasp, and removing any splinters or loose pieces, and shortening the toe ; and not cutting away any of the frog, but merely removing any rough or stringy pieces.

Do not cut the sole away until you can spring it with your thumbs, for if you do you will take away the only protection the foot has against rough roads and inclement weather. You will wonder why the horse is lame and restless on his feet (even in the stable). It is because you have cut too much of the sole away. This is a great mistake many horseshoers make, who, imagining they cannot hurt the foot by trying to make it look nice and clean, sometimes cut until the blood comes. This is wrong ; as the sole is the natural protection for that part of the foot, it must be left as near its natural condition as possible, thereby saving the foot from contraction ; for it is quite reasonable, if you cut out the sole you weaken the sides, causing them to draw in.

Do not cut away the frog until you have struck the quick or sensitive frog—you might as well cut the skin from the sole of your own feet and try to walk on rough roads, or wear rough shoes without stockings. Let it remain in its natural condition, *let it touch the ground;* do not try to make it look neat by cutting away a most valuable supporter of the foot and leg, causing the hoof to lose its proper shape at the heels. I contend that *the frog must touch the ground* in order to fulfill its duty, to support the foot and prevent contraction, for while it does there can be no contraction, and it is the *only* remedy for contraction.

Do not open up the heel, as it is worse than cutting away the frog—it is a support for the heel, and if cut out it causes a weakness of the walls of the hoof and will cause contraction of the heel. Merely shorten the toe and level the foot and proceed with fitting the shoe.—*By* J. R.

Dressing the Foot.

One of the great and most important features of horseshoeing is the dressing of the foot. In performing this

Fig. 61.—Showing Foot ready for the Shoe.

operation it is first very important that the tools employed in paring be in good condition. It is hardly necessary to say that judgment is required, as some feet grow more rapidly at the toe and others at the heel. Remove the dead hoof from the sole of the foot, being very particular to let the frog bars stand on either side ; then remove the horn of the foot, and rasp down level. Do not pare the frog, for if you do the tender parts will be exposed, and it will soon become very hard and unhealthy, and cause the foot to contract. In Fig. 61 I have endeavored to show a foot ready to receive the shoe.

Another important matter is the fitting. The shoe should in every instance be fitted to the foot and not the foot to the shoe. Heat the shoe so that in applying it will mark the un-

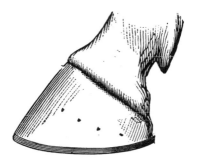

Fig. 62.—Showing Best Position for Nails.

even surface (if any there be), which should then be removed. Do not heat it red-hot and burn the foot down level, as that renders the horn very brittle. Having the shoe fitted, it is now ready to be nailed on. The nails should be given a good hold in the sound hoof. The heel nail on the front foot should be driven the lowest ; the second a little higher ; the third and the fourth also a little higher than the preceding ones, as indicated in Fig. 62.

The shoe being driven on, the next important point is to draw the nails tightly to prevent the clinches from raising above the foot and the shoe getting loose. After this has been done, the foot is ready to receive the finishing touches, which should be performed in a neat manner by filing the clinch thin and turning down, care being taken not to file a gutter under the clinches. I have often seen a foot that deep gutters have been filed in crack open and shell off. After the clinches have been turned down, rasp off the superfluous hoof even with the shoe, but be careful not to rasp above the nail.—*By* TOE KNIFE.

Preparing the Foot for Shoeing—Interfering—Forging—Hot and Cold Fitting—Split Hoofs.

I am a practical horseshoer and not a writer. What I have to offer is from experience.

In an article like this I cannot enter into the anatomy of the horse's foot, even if I had a profound knowledge of it, which I confess I have not.

On a foot that is about to be shod it is necessary to remove the horn to a level with the sole at its outer margin at the toe, and at the heels low enough to obtain the desired angle, which varies considerably in different horses. It should be kept as near the natural condition as possible. The sole should not be touched with knife or rasp as a general practice, and it may be made to support a part of the horse's weight by having the shoe rest on a portion of the sole equal to the thickness of the wall. The frog should never be touched with a knife, except to remove pieces that may have become partly detached by exfoliation and remain flapping on the foot. In such cases, it is better to remove these loose pieces, as the foot is very sensitive to the touch.

A shoe adapted to the foot should be selected, and it must be fitted as accurately as possible, and not, as is often practised by shoers, fitted by making the shoe a little smaller, and rasping the foot to fit the shoe.   This is one of the worst habits of shoers, and is undoubtedly the cause of nine-tenths of the hard, brittle feet we meet with.

The reason for this is plain. The hoof is covered with an epidermis or cuticle of silicious material which, when destroyed, enables the moisture naturally contained in the hoof to evaporate too rapidly, causing the hoof to become hard, dry and brittle, and with a little help from a faulty shoe, such a foot is eventually likely to enter that state of wide-spread deformity styled contraction.

The shoe should be attached with as small nails as prac-ticable, and as few as will be sufficient to retain it, never nailing far back on the inside quarter, so as to allow the heels to expand.   Some shoers are in favor of punching the holes in such a position that the nails may be driven through the middle of the wall, but I obtain a firmer hold, with less liability to fracture the wall, by starting the nail at the inside of the wall, and driving it obliquely upward and outward.

The nail should be of the best material, should fit snug in the shoe, and the clinches should be short and well ham-mered down.

Interference is a very common annoyance, but easily pre-vented if the cause is properly understood. Interfering may almost always be prevented by removing the portion of the shoe which does the injury. This may be ascertain-ed by applying a boot covered with paint, and trotting the horse until a part of the paint becomes attached to the op-posite shoe, which will show the exact spot which does the mischief.   Some horses have malformation of the legs, which predispose them to interfere. I have cured some such horses by rasping the outside quarter back to the heel quite thin, but never resort to this plan when I can substi-tute another, as it is apt to weaken the quarter and alter the gait of the horse. One side of the foot should never be raised higher than the other, on account of the undue strain which will be brought to bear upon the ligaments, and the natural pressure upon the blood vessels and secretory apparatus upon the highest side prevents them from performing their natural functions, and another evil may be developed as bad as interfering.

Forging is a very annoying habit which may be prevented by making the web of the front shoe narrow and sloping the edge of the toe off, the hind shoe backward when calkings are not employed. Forging is caused by the edge of the hind shoe striking against the inner edge of the front shoe as the hind foot is descending to its place, and when the front foot is raised and about to be carried forward. The method indicated will allow the front part of the hind shoe to strike the sole or frog of the front foot and obviate the noise or click. It may also be prevented by using weighted shoes. Calkins are a benefit to the shoe but are objectionable for the foot. They cause the shoe to wear longer, and will secure a surer footing for a draft horse on some kinds of ground, but their recommendation ends there. The greatest objections I have to calkins is the distance which they remove the frog from the ground. The frog in its natural condition is almost on a level with the lower edge of the wall, and helps to sustain the weight of the horse, which would otherwise be borne by the laminæ which connects the coffin bone to the wall. With calkins the laminæ can sustain the weight, but the frog cannot perform its functions. When the frog can come in contact with the ground it acts like a spring, preventing concussion, and when pressed hard it expands the foot. Calkins furthermore increase the leverage and impose unnecessary strain on the nails, and should not be employed when they can be dispensed with.

Hot and cold fittings both have their advocates. I am entirely in favor of hot fitting ; *red hot*, and not a *black hot*. After the shoe is fitted, heat it red hot and press it to the foot and remove it instantly ; if there are any inequalities they appear, and should be removed with a rasp, and the shoe again pressed to the foot as before, until a perfectly level bearing is obtained. A hot shoe applied for two or three seconds to the foot cannot injure it, as it only affects the part presented for wear and tear, and that in a very beneficial manner by hardening it, and rendering it less liable to the action of moisture. A more accurate bearing can be obtained by hot fitting than by any other method. A small, narrow clip, judiciously placed, is desirable for roadsters.

The manner in which I treat split hoof with the best success is as follows : I make a shoe rather wider in the web than usual. Then draw up a solid clip inside of the extreme ends of the branches so as to fit on the inside of the bars ; punch a nail hole in the end of each branch, then weaken the shoe directly under the split. If the split be at the toe, a clip may be placed on each side of the toe. Clean out the split with some small instrument, and nail on with strong nails, not driven too tight at the heels. Then spread the shoe until the crack is nearly closed. It will not require much spreading, as the shoe will bend directly under the split. No cutting or burning should be done, but some stimulating ointment that would keep the skin soft, applied to the coronet would be beneficial.

Shoes of all horses cannot be the same, and it is hard to recommend any certain form of shoe to be used generally. A shoe should be as light as the nature of the horse's labor will admit. A heavier shoe cannot possibly benefit the foot, and it imposes a vast amount of unnecessary labor upon the animal; far more, indeed, than we are apt to suppose, until we observe how often a horse raises his feet in a given time. Then by multiplying that by the weight of the shoe, one can see what an enormous weight is raised by a horse in a few hours' traveling and that, too, in a very disadvantageous manner, it being raised as with a lever, with the weight on the long end.—*By* J. C. BUCK.

The True Way to Shoe Horses.

While there have been great improvements in almost everything else during the past quarter of a century, I have noticed little, if any, improvement in horseshoeing.

I started to learn the blacksmith's trade in 1858, and have never done anything else. I claim to be expert at all kinds of carriage-work and horseshoeing. Some people say that a carriage-ironer cannot know how to shoe a horse. I can give you the names of hundreds of our best citizens who will testify to my capacity as a horseshoer, and after you have read about my method you can judge for yourself.

For the past eighteen years I have been constantly shoeing horses, and have learned the ways of several States and Canada, and I assert positively that there is only one way to shoe a horse so that he will travel easy and at the same time keep the hoof sound. Some may say that all horses cannot be shod in the same way, but I claim they can. Allow me to describe the method I use, and I believe you will agree with me in the statement just made. If the following instructions are carefully followed the result will be satisfactory in every case.

First, I take a good sixteen-inch rasp and rasp down the foot level, watching that the heels are not cut down too low. After the foot is trimmed to the proper shape, I use a knife to smooth it, and never cut the braces of the foot, for they are the strength of it; and never use the knife on the frog, for it is the heart of the foot. The frog sheds off once in two or three months, when the foot is in a healthy condition. The frog is intended for a cushion, and the larger it is the better. When a horse trots he always strikes the heels to the ground first, and if he has a large frog exposed to strike first it will naturally lessen the jar to the leg, and operate to keep the heels well spread. On the other hand, if the frog is cut out, what is left becomes dry, so dry that it cannot be cut with a knife, and the heels shrink together.

After having trimmed the feet, as I have stated, to the proper size, I select a shoe just large enough to cover the foot, and then shape it to fit. Applying it to the hoof, I watch that the hoof is scorched only just enough to show the unevenness of the foot, and then with a rasp or knife smooth true. In this way I never fail to fit a shoe properly. If the shoe is fitted correctly, the heels are always well spread out. If the shoes are too long the heels will be drawn together, and the foot, being thus pinched, becomes contracted, and results in a lame horse.

Next, the shoes should always be concaved on the fore feet. Never put hind shoes on the fore feet. The shoe should bear only on the outer rim of the hoof, and watch that it bears equally all around, and not simply on the toe and heel. If these directions are followed, the horse will never be troubled with lameness in the feet, caused by improper shoeing. If the shoe is not left on more than sixty days, bruises or corns cannot form in the hoof.

Now a word about driving nails, and I have done. Nails should never be driven high, and then in six or eight weeks the foot will have grown sufficiently to enable the shoer to cut out the old nail-holes, leaving sound hoofs. If the nails, however, are driven high, at the next shoeing, the hoof will not have grown enough to cut down to the old nail-holes, and the water and mud will soak into these old holes and cause the hoof to become rotten and brittle.

I will guarantee satisfaction in all cases, and I furthermore say that deformed feet can be remodeled and cured under my treatment.—*By* A. LAROCK.

Shoeing for Sound Feet.

Horseshoeing should be done in such a manner as to keep healthy, sound feet in their natural condition, and to make unhealthy ones as near sound as possible. I have been especially interested in the theories bought forward on the question of "Hot *vs.* Cold Fitting." Some make it very plain that if hot fitting is practised it is sure to ruin the horse. Others again show clearly that cold fitting is almost as injurious, and entails the extra drawback of waste of time.

It seems to me that a combination of the two methods would bring better results than either would alone. I advocate hot fitting and cold practice ; that is, fit the shoe hot, and scarcely touch the foot with it, and when the foot is sore or diseased don't even touch it, but bring the shoe close enough to it to enable you to shape it to the foot, instead of fitting the foot to the shoe. Of course in diseased feet we cannot always fit the shoe to the foot, but we can fit the shoe as nearly as possible to where the foot ought to be, using the frog for a center guide.

Horseshoeing is a trade that needs good judgment and a large amount of practical common sense, as each horse is different from all others, and we might say that each foot on the same horse is different from the other three. Each individual foot must be shod according to its peculiarities or disease. Hence the impossibility of making any one rule that will answer for all horses. Even those afflicted with the same trouble will often require different treatment. "One man's meat is another man's poison," is a saying that applies to horses as well as to men.

In paring the foot cut only the dead horn away, and on no condition pare the sole, but with your knife scrape out the loose and dead layers, if there are any. Our object should be to assist nature against the unnatural wear to which the foot is subjected and not to try to improve on a healthy foot.

Fit the foot true and let it stand squarely on the floor. If the horse interferes do not cut one side of the foot more, cant the foot, twist the ankle and throw the whole limb out of balance, but keep it true and in balance and fit the shoe to stop the interfering. There are but few cases of interfering that cannot be cured with proper feed, care, and driving in connection with shoeing. If the shoe and foot are fitted true, as they should be, there will be a true, even bearing all around the wall. Bring the heels of the shoe in, so that the point of the wall where it joins the bar will rest on the shoe. Do not spread the heels wide to avoid pinching or contraction of the foot. The wide heels and high calks—as far as shoeing is responsible for contracted feet—cause more of them than all other methods put together. The wide heels and high calks leave a point of horn to come down between the heels of the shoe and prevent the natural action of the foot. In shoeing contracted feet make the inside of the shoe heels the highest, or level them out, so that every time the horse steps it tends to spread the foot. Use as few and as small nails as possible, and secure the shoe firmly in its place. In winter use as light calkins as are consistent with the use of the horse, and in summer put none at all on driving horses at least, and if a common sense shoe like the "Juniata" is used, flat on the top and concave on the bottom, many team horses can haul heavier loads and do it easier than they can on calkins.

In shoeing a spavined horse keep the toe low, and use a very long shoe with high heels on the spavined leg, as the horse has partly or entirely lost the use of the hock joint. The method will make the horse travel much easier and greatly relieve the lameness.

I do not believe in the so-called spring heels ; I regard them as a positive injury to the foot. To illustrate : A few days ago a horse came to my shop with one front shoe bent nearly an inch. The horse had been driven about thirty miles since he stepped on the shoe. After taking the shoe off I found the foot twisted about three-fourths of an inch. Now, if in traveling thirty miles one-quarter of the foot can be driven past the other three-fourths of an inch, so as to rest on a twisted shoe, why will not the foot, instead of the shoe, do the springing when the so-called spring heels are used ? The shoe being nailed at the toe, when the horse puts his foot down it makes a lever purchase, and the heaviest pressure comes on the weakest part of the foot, the heel quarter, where the wall is the thinnest, and receives the least support.—*By* YANKEE BLACKSMITH.

For Hot Fitting.

I believe it was about the year 1840, that a certain Mr. Riquet, a veterinary surgeon, introduced what was termed a " podometrical " method of shoeing. From the time the method of fitting shoes to the hoof was introduced, a few inexperienced and professional men imagined that injury was done to the horse's foot. In rare cases this was the fact, for the custom was to pare the hoof down almost to the quick. So that we cannot wonder that a few careless workmen would press the hot shoe so long upon the hoof as to permit the border of the sensitive sole to suffer from the high temperature. These accidents appear, however, to have been infrequent, as we read of very few cases of this kind.

The idea prevails to some extent, that hot fitting is hurtful, and it was to guard against this that the "podometer" was invented. This instrument was devised for the purpose of taking the dimensions of the foot. It was ingenious, but deficient, as it took the exact size, but not the shape of the foot. The size of the foot was then entered in a register, and sent to the forge, where the shoes were forged according to the measure of the foot after it had been pared down. Now, it seems as though anyone could drive the shoe on, when the horse was in the stable or on the highway; certainly such shoes could not fit as though the impression had been made by a heated shoe. The trouble is that when the hoof is pared down and the cold shoe placed thereon, more or less cavities will remain between the hoof and shoe, so that the hoof does not rest equally on the shoe. By hot fitting, of course, a perfect fit can be secured. When the shoe is applied hot, the action of the heat on the hoof has a tendency to soften the hoof, so that when the nail is driven in, it can be driven more easily and accurately ; and as the hoof cools, it contracts about the nails and holds them firmly in their places, as shown by the following :

" At the Cavalry School of Saumur, in an experiment covering an interval of over three years, from September 22, 1841, to October 5, 1844, all the near-sided horses of the school were shod by the cold, and the off-sided ones by the hot method. In that space of time, out of 22,579 horses that were fitted in the cold state, 386 shoes were lost, detached or broken, and only 123 out of the same number were lost, that were fitted while hot. That is, in the first case one shoe in 58 was detached, while in the second case one shoe out of 103 was lost. This great difference would have been still greater if the hot method had been practised in the ordinary manner. But the school was then laboring under an impression developed by the Podometric System, that there was danger of burning the sole, and an order was given to the farriers to apply the hot shoes very lightly, and to remove that part of the hoof which had been in contact with the shoe. This was almost a return to the cold method of fitting.

Colonel Ambert, also of the Saumur School, observed that, out of 600 horses, from 55 to 60 lost their shoes every month during the employment of cold fitting, or in other words, the regiment lost a shoe every hour they marched, while with the system of hot fitting the regiment lost only one shoe in eight days.

After careful observation and many experiments, I have come to the conclusion that hot fitting is not attended with any danger when properly practised, and that hot shoeing, as practised at that time, allows the workmen to make the shoe to fit the foot, an advantage that the cold shoeing does not possess. In fact, all the most distinguished veterinary professors or practitioners who have studied the subject, have unhesitatingly given the preference to hot fitting.— *By* FRANK I. GILBERT.

Favors Hot Fitting for Oxen.

A person who has practised cold fitting all his life, of course thinks no other system is right, and is apt to regard the advocates of hot fitting as being greatly in the dark. He feels quite sure that the animals subjected to such barbarous and cruel treatment will be certainly ruined.

Now, what is the object in fitting a shoe hot? I answer, to get a perfect and solid bearing which can be obtained in no other way, as every smith well knows. Again I inquire, Why is so perfect a fit desirable? The only answer that can be given is, because the shoe will then stay upon the foot much longer than it otherwise would. But is it a fact that shoes hot fitted will stay on much longer than those cold fitted? We claim that such is the case. This matter has been thoroughly tested, with the most satisfactory results in favor of hot fitting. Some think hot fitting rots the hoof and makes it brittle, and tell us that some horses have had their feet so injured by hot fitting that their shoes could not be kept on a week. I don't doubt this statement, for I know very well that there are many bunglers connected with the trade that never ought to be allowed to meddle with a horse's foot; and I unhesitatingly affirm that nine-tenths of the evils supposed to be the result of hot fitting can be traced directly or indirectly to the incompetency or carelessness of the shoer. That there are dangers attending the hot-fitting system, which should be carefully guarded against, I frankly admit. Horses and oxen are often lamed through gross carelessness on the part of the shoer. A smith who will pare the foot down so near the quick that it will readily yield under the pressure of the thumb and then press the hot shoe upon it, and hold it there until it is imbedded into the foot the whole thickness of the shoe, causing the animal to spring and cringe, deserves the severest censure and ought to leave the business. I will now give my way of hot fitting in shoeing cattle. For horses I seldom fit the shoes hot, it not being necessary, as they stay on quite long enough if put on cold, but with oxen it is different.

In preparing the foot I use neither butteris nor knife, but instead a sharp rasp. I rasp the foot down level, but not so much that it will give under thumb-pressure. In applying the hot shoe I am careful to see that it does not remain on the

foot over two seconds at a time. It should be raised a
little two or three times during the operation, in order that
the cold air may keep the heat from penetrating to the
quick. As soon as an impression is obtained I remove the
shoe. I also burn in the clinches. This has been my method
of shoeing cattle for many years, and I have gained a reputa-
tion for making shoes "hang on" better than any cold fitter can claim in my vicinity. Furthermore, I have seen no
rotten or brittle hoofs. Another advantage gained in hot
fitting is that the heat has a tendency to soften the hoof, and
this allows nails to be driven more easily and accurately in
cold weather. To sum the matter up, I believe that no bad
effect can result from hot fitting if the work is properly
done.—*By* W. H. B.

Favors Hot Fitting.

The reasons given for cold fitting are about as follows :

1. "That burning the hoof seems unnatural, closing its
pores, tending to keep the hoof dry," etc., and that "hot
fitting" is adopted because it is a quicker method.

2. "Hot fitting stops the pores ; it kills the nerves and
fibre ; the foot is made brittle ; the shoe will get loose
sooner ; the sole of the foot will separate from the inner
hoof about once a year ; the foot is made tender and the
horse lamed for life ;" all of which, if true, would certainly
furnish sufficient reasons for abandoning the practice for-
ever.

Now, from these opinions, backed up as I know they are
by many writers upon the subject, both ancient and modern, I, with all due respect, must beg leave to dissent. The
position I take is this, that "hot fitting" is not only the
quickest but that it is the best method. By "hot fitting"
I do not mean to burn away for several minutes to save

cutting, but after the foot is properly prepared to apply the hot shoe for a moment, then remove and use the knife to remove the inequalities. Then apply the shoe until the whole surface has been seared, and this takes but an instant's application of the hot shoe. If the foot has been properly prepared, and the shoe is of the right size and shape, we shall have that most desirable thing—a perfect fit, but more important than even that, we shall by the hot iron have closed the pores of the horn and thus prevented the escape of the moisture which nature provides for this living structure. I want to emphasize this fact that the hoof is a living structure, nourished and supplied with all that is necessary for its growth and health from the inside; that is, in a healthy foot. In the case of the animal running in the field without shoes, the hoof is worn or bruised off, keeping the pores closed, upon the same plan upon which the écraseur operates in severing blood vessels; but in cutting the hoof we leave these pores exposed, and the nearer we cut to the sensitive parts the greater number we expose, the more moisture will escape, and the greater injury we shall inflict.

Now just here the best reason for "hot fitting" comes in. By touching lightly the cut surface we seal up the avenues by which moisture escapes, and thus prevent the drying of the horn. This theory can be easily tested. Let anyone take the knife and rasp and pare the foot in the ordinary way and fit the shoe cold, and then take another foot of the same animal and pare and fit the shoe hot, and after the lapse of a few hours remove the shoes. The burned hoof will have a hard, thin crust upon it, and just under this it will be as moist as when cut, but the other one will be found hard and dry for a considerable depth.

This burning counteracts the evil of the unnatural process of cutting the hoof.

How anyone who has given the subject thought can believe that it is injurious to touch the hot shoe to the superfluous horn upon the bottom of the hoof, horn which has served its purpose and would be entirely worn away were the animal to go barefooted for a short time, considering, too, the fact that horn is a non-conductor of heat, passes my comprehension.

I am satisfied that the evils attributed to "hot fitting" are due to other causes which only the most thorough knowledge of the physiology and anatomy of the parts, and a long experience will reveal.

The business of shoeing and managing horses' feet so as to preserve soundness and restore those which have become ill-shapen and diseased, is one whose importance can scarcely be overestimated.—*By* E. A. McLELLAN.

Against Hot Fitting.

I cannot see why anyone is in favor of hot fitting, unless it is easier done. It surely is not because a hot shoe is beneficial to the hoof. Do you think that you can take a hot shoe and burn a bearing without injury to the hoof?

Heat is one of the worst enemies of the health and toughness of a horse's hoof. I never saw a hoof that had been subjected to hot fitting for any length of time that was not greatly damaged, being hard, dry and brittle. You cannot apply a hot shoe to a horse's hoof without injury. If the foot is flat or thin it will stand very little heat, and at any rate you are working on dangerous ground. A foot dressed with nippers, knife and rasp to a level bearing, and shoe properly fitted and nailed, has none of the above objections. —*By* R. T.

Against Hot Fitting.

Hot fitting is a barbarous practice ; it draws the oil and moisture from the foot and leaves it crisp and brittle. I have seen smiths hold a red-hot shoe on a foot until it has been fried like a steak.

Why is this done ?

Because they are too lazy to use the knife and rasp. A smith is justified in heating a shoe hot enough to make an impression on the foot, but no hotter, and a smith who cannot fit a shoe in this way ought to leave the business. I do not think that any rules from books can be of much use to shoers, because a style of shoeing that will answer well for one horse may not do at all for the next. I think horseshoeing requires more study than any other part of the smith's trade.—*By* U. B.

Cold Fitting Best.

I notice that a few smiths are not yet alive to the absurdity of hot fitting. I regard the practice as unworthy of civilized men. My way is to keep on hand shoes of every shape and size likely to be called for, and by doing this I avoid the necessity for heating while shoeing. Keep a sharp butteris for trimming feet, and get a nice fit without burning.

Time and coal are lost in reheating, and, moreover, the shoe must be made quite hot, so that it may burn the outside quickly without heating the foot more than is necessary. But when the shoe has cooled it will not fit the impression in the hoof, because the iron has, of course, shrunk. So that, after all, burning will not make a shoe level. I can put a shoe on by the time a man who burns is ready to drive the first nail.

Perhaps some men are fond of burning because they have

no skill in using the butteris or knife. It requires a good
deal of practice to use these tools properly, but any boy or
clumsy old farmer can burn a foot.

I don't know how this idea of hot fitting originated, but it
is about on a par with the practice of Indians in burning
away the surplus wood in shaving tools and implements.
There was a time, too, when farmers burned logs instead of
sawing them ; but that was long ago. Farmers don't burn
logs now. Yet it is just as sensible to do so as to apply
a red-hot shoe to a horse's hoof. Let the man who believes
in putting a hot shoe on within three-eighths of an inch of
live flesh and blood try the experiment of placing a hot
horse-nail head on his big toe nail, and allowing it to remain
there until its shape is well defined on the nail. I think he
would then discover that hot fitting was not such a brilliant
idea as he had imagined.

Another objection to burning a hoof is that it causes an
offensive smell and smoke, and makes the horse jerk and
twist so that it is a wonder some smiths don't get kicked to
death.—*By* F. B.

Against Hot Fitting.

It is well known to all horseshoers that many horses'
feet, particularly the front ones, and especially in summer
time, are very hard and brittle, and about as difficult to cut
as a cow's horn. Now, if a red-hot shoe is held to a horse's
hoof for a few seconds the hoof can be immediately cut as
easily as a piece of mellow cheese. Mind what I say, the
foot is always cut instantly after the burning, or there is
nothing gained by the operation. This alone is the reason
why hot fitters follow the practice, and anything else that
is said about it is merely a waste of words, intended to mis-
lead. The word cold fitting is a misnomer, for there is no
such thing. All shoes are fitted to the horses' feet while the

shoes are hot. As the shoe is worked on the anvil, so it is fitted or formed to the foot. It is impossible to fit a shoe to a horse's foot without scorching the foot a little, or if possible, no man would take the trouble with a cold shoe for the very good reason " That the devil gets the smith that hammers cold iron."

But to do as some smiths do, hold a red-hot shoe to a horse's foot until the smoke of the burning hoof actually hides the smith, is barbarous in the extreme. Doubtless there are some honest, well-meaning, but very hard-worked horseshoers that quiet their consciences by the thought that burning the hoofs does the horse little or no harm, and enables them to do more and easier work. With all due deference to these men, I say most emphatically, the practice is one of the most injurious to which a horse can be subjected.

It is all nonsense to say that horseshoes cannot be made to stay on and wear as well by cold fitting as by hot fitting. I have seen horses shod by cold fitting, and the shoes have remained on over three months and done well all that time, and the horses were working every day, Sundays excepted. I do not advocate any such thing, however, for in my opinion six weeks is a long enough time for shoes to stay on any horse's feet.

In conclusion I will say, if all horse owners would insist that there must be no more burning of their horses' feet when shod (even if something more must be paid for the work), the practice would cease but not till then.—*By* M. D. D.

CHAPTER V.

CONTRACTED FEET.

Contraction probably gives shoers more trouble than any other one thing connected with shoeing. In greater or less degree contraction is present in a large percentage of feet. The good shoer is constantly employed in an effort to guard against it, and if horse owners were as intelligent as they ought to be, and careful to exercise that intelligence, he would, more frequently than he does, succeed in reducing the difficulty to a minimum. The different methods employed by shoers to overcome this trouble are presented in this chapter.

Causes of Contraction.

Perhaps there is no more prolific source of lameness in the horse than contraction, which simply means a gradual loosening of the entire hoof, chiefly in the heel, and for some reason or other, generally of the fore feet. It is commonly called by horsemen "widening of the hoof," and pressing unduly upon the sensitive laminæ of the hoof, produces that peculiar lameness which so much puzzles the uninitiated, being to them an invisible cause. Even the so-called horse-doctors are generally completely puzzled by this disease when looking for the cause of lameness. There is no possible criterion for fixing the appearance accurately of any peculiarity of lameness consequent upon contraction—sometimes the lameness being very slight, while at other times it is very acute, so much so as to render the horse for the time quite useless, being generally pronounced foundered by those who think they know whereof they speak.

Its causes are numerous and various ; but, in my opinion, which is founded upon practical observation, the chief cause is in faulty shoeing. Sufficient attention is not paid to the nature of the hoof to be shod ; a thin shell hoof requires a light shoe ; the nails should be small, and not too tightly clinched. This last point is very important indeed, in all shoeing, yet a horse with a strong, thick hoof, may take a much heavier shoe and larger nails, and they may be a little more tightly clinched.

Another very important point for which the blacksmith is not answerable, is that some persons, farmers especially, allow the shoes to be worn just as long as they will stay on, often letting a poor horse do hard work with three, two, or even one shoe on. By this means horses are quite apt to have one hoof larger than the other, from the fact that the bare foot, or feet, wear down, while the ones shod retain all the hoof, hence the cause for the remark so common, "your horse has odd feet." It is a good plan to allow horses to go barefoot a few days occasionally ; by so doing the hoof expands, and so far is a preventive of contraction. Foul, dirty stables, or other manure heaps, occasion the disease by the action of ammonia upon the horny portion of the feet.

Standing constantly upon a hard, dry floor is another source of this evil also. Such horses should have woolen pads or cloths of several thicknesses tied loosely around, just above and overhanging the hoof, which are to be kept constantly wet with water. Finally, if the feet are very bad, take off all the shoes, open the heels on each side of the cleft of the frog, pare until you can see the quick, and, if grass time, turn him out in a damp pasture ; if not grass' time, turn him in the next similar and best place you can for a few weeks, and you will be more likely to effect a cure. When he is taken up, care must be taken not to subject him to the same causes. If the horse should be still lame after the paring, as he will be, do not be afraid, he will soon get over it, and be all the more sound for the paring as recommended.—WM. HORNE, V. S., *in Dixie Farmer*.

Shoeing Contracted Feet.

In shoeing for contraction I take a spreader, made of ¼-inch round iron, sharpen it at both ends, bend the points back about one-quarter of an inch to a square band, and then bend it into the shape of a clevis with both points straight out. I next pare the hoof down well, and if there is any inflammation in it, I pour some turpentine on the bottom, set fire to it and let it burn, but not long enough to allow the hoof to become dry anywhere. I then extinguish the fire with a rag, and bend the spreader so as to fit in between the heels of the hoof, but leaving it wider than the heels by as much as I wish to spread the hoof. I then put one end of the spreader on one heel and pry the other end down with a punch or piece of iron. Next I nail on the shoe and mix up a lotion composed of one ounce of corrosive sublimate, finely pulverized, and one pint of turpentine. This should be put in a strong bottle and applied to the foot at intervals until the inflammation has disappeared. Then the shoe should be removed, and a piece of leather, on which pine tar has been spread, should be placed on the bottom of the hoof. The shoe must then be nailed on again carefully, and the spreader applied to it Next I take one part of soft soap made of potash, one of lard and one of turpentine; stir well together and use for softening the hoof and stimu-

lating its growth.   This plan has never failed with me yet.
—*By* C. K. S.

Shoeing Contracted Feet.

To shoe for contracted feet I pare the toe down all I dare,
leaving the heel as high as I can ; then, in fitting the shoe,

Fig. 63—Showing a Shoe made by a Common but Faulty Method.

instead of turning the heel in as a good many smiths do, I
turn it out and nail the shoe on in the ordinary way.   But

Fig. 64—Proper form of Shoe for Contracted Feet.

when this is done, I take a pair of tongs, and, placing them
between the heels, spread the heels just a little.   This will

spread the foot if it is repeated each time the horse is shod.
The reason I turn the heels out is that when turned in, as
in Fig. 63 of the annexed engravings, the bearing is brought
so close together that the weight pressing outside of the
bearings draws the shoe together. But if you turn the
heels out, as in Fig. 64, you get a broad bearing that
will not draw together. I turn the heels out on all the
shoes I put on, and find that the plan always gives satisfaction.—*By* C. S. E.

Proper Shoeing for Contracted Feet.

Contracted feet are more commonly the consequence of
lameness in horses than the cause. Any diseased condition
inside the hoof giving rise to an unusual degree of heat
leads to a more rapid evaporation from the surface of the
horn, to drying and shrinking of the hoof, and to absorp-
tion of the soft parts within. The shrinkage or narrowing
takes place especially at the heel, where the foot has not a
long, but only an elastic, cartilaginous internal support,
which yields easily to any pressure from without.

A second condition, which always coincides with this drying due to disease, is the disease of the heel caused by the
animal standing on its toe, or removing the weight from
the entire foot. When the foot is planted on the ground
and the weight thrown upon it, the soft parts descending
within the hoof tend to press it outward, and as a matter of
fact the hoof does actually expand at the upper part,
next the hair, and thus the natural tendency of the unused
elastic horn to contract is to a great extent counteracted.
Disease is, therefore, a more common cause of contraction,
and in all cases of contracted feet it is well first to look for
some existing disease, such as corns, bruises, pricks, and
other wounds, graveling, thrush, inflammation from uneven

bearing of the shoe, from the nails being drawn up too tight, from navicular disease, from ringbone affecting the second or third phalanx, and so on.

Apart from any disease sufficient to cause lameness, contraction of the feet sometimes goes on to an extreme degree, until, indeed, one heel may meet the other ; yet lameness is not induced. Yet, if contraction takes place with rapidity, as under the influence of a long period of rainless weather following a wet spring, the compression of the soft parts by the drying and shrinking horn will cause inflammation and lameness. Contraction caused in this way may be counteracted and corrected by measures calculated to soften and expand the horn, followed by such as will retain its natural moisture and give proper bearing on the shoe. To soften the contracted foot, keep the unshod animal standing every day for sixteen hours in a stream of water coming up to the hair around the top of the hoof, or in a soft muck of clay puddle, closing in around the foot to the same level. In frosty weather a warm poultice, placed in a strong bag drawn over the foot, is preferable, the more so that it can be kept applied night and day. At the end of a fortnight the foot will usually be found to have expanded to its natural dimensions.

If there is much lameness, it will be desirable to apply a blister on the front and sides of the pastern during the period of poulticing. This may be repeated and the poulticing continued, if lameness remains at the end of a fortnight. As a blister, the following may be rubbed into the skin on the front and sides of the pastern : Powdered cantharides, one-half drachm ; oil of lavender, ten drops ; olive oil one ounce. It may be repeated the second day if heat and tenderness have not been induced by the first application and also so soon as the effects of the first application have passed off and the resulting scabs have dropped off.

When lameness has disappeared, and the foot has been sufficiently expended. it should be dressed carefully, going the same height to the wall at all corresponding points on the inner and outer sides, and paring heel and toe in proper ratio with each other, the sole being left as far as possible to come to the heel with the hoof wall at all points, and furnish with it a surface of bearing for the shoe.

The shoe should be perfectly loose and smooth, and when applied should press evenly at all points. It should be drawn only moderately tight, and on giving its final dress-

Fig. 65—Proper Way of Driving Nails.

ing the use of the file should be as far as possible avoided. The horn is formed of a series of pus tubes with an inter-tubular cellular structure, and when the rasp or file is used so as to expose the open ends of these tubules the contained moisture exhales, the horn withers, and the soft parts may be injuriously pressed upon. For this reason the use of the file on the front of the hoof is to be severely deprecated. It should only be used on the lower edge of the hoof wall, where it projects over the shoe, and when the sharp edges might otherwise split up. For a similar reason the sole should never be pared down into the tough, elastic horn, though all scaly masses on the surface may be safely removed.   After shaving, the use of hoof ointment will serve to prevent evaporation and drying, and is absolutely needful after the foot has been softened by poulticing.   A mixture of equal parts of wood tar and sweet oil will answer admirably.   This brushed daily over the entire surface of the horn—wall, sole and frog—will usually preserve a suf-

Fig. 66—A Faulty Method of Driving Nails.

ficiency of moisture and the natural elasticity and toughness of the horn.—PROF. LAW *in Farmer's Gazette.*

Shoeing Contracted Feet.

My method of shoeing for contracted feet, is as follows : I make a shoe to fit the foot nicely all around and trim the foot as much as it will bear, taking care to keep it as level as possible and not to disturb the frog or interfere with the bridge.   I then put the shoe on the foot and drive in all the nails, bending them up against the foot instead of breaking them off or bending them down as some men do. After these nails are all driven I draw them out again, spread the shoe all around one-eighth of an inch and drive the nails back in the same holes. This gently draws the hoof apart and eases the pressure on the pedal bones. The nails being driven inward tend to spread the foot. Every time the horse steps on a shoe made on my plan, and shown in Fig. 65 of the engravings annexed, the foot will be drawn apart, but a shoe made and put on in the manner illustrated in Fig. 66 will draw the foot together. In following my method it is necessary to remove the shoe from the horse every ten or fourteen days and let him stand on a dampened dirt floor. Under this treatment he will soon be cured.—*By* R. J. G.

Contracted Feet, Corns, and Chest Founder.

Relative to shoeing chest-foundered horses, and in regard to contracted feet and corns, I will say that the three, although called by different names, belong to the same family, and all are in the foot, chest founder not excepted. And I still insist upon it as logical. Now, who will undertake to say that a horse's breast has become shrunken from its natural make up, in any respect, except from the loss of flesh, or by being poor ; the bone or brisket is all there ; none of it has been taken out ; just set the feet back under the horse, and he will have just as full a breast as he ever had, excepting he may be poorer in flesh. Now, what is the fact about a contracted foot or any other foot ? As a rule, the frog is not only the cushion on which the horse stands, but is the width of heel, also. Now, if the frog is small, unnaturally hard or diseased from any cause, usually you will find the shell of heel and bars narrowing in, and, it is said, true enough, that the foot is contracted ; the angle of the heel hooks into the frog, and needs separating ; the shell of the foot sets on to the wing of the paddle bone, and we get corns here, and the result is, in either case, a sore foot, like the result of a tight, stiff boot full of wrinkles, pegs and nails, and the feet are set out in front to rest and ease the pressure of weight, the shoulders set forward, and the breast looks as if it had been driven in, and is improperly called chest founder.

Now, to pull the heel open is to pull the bars away from the frog; if it is spread enough to do any good, it hurts, whether done with nailing tongs, screws or a stump puller; and what fills this cavity made by pulling the heel open, except the frog, and of course you must wait for the frog to grow to accomplish it, and the horse must endure this torture to accommodate faulty practices. Now just let the horse have a ground bearing on the frog, and keep the frog and hoof soft and cool with water, so that it won't hurt the horse to stand on the frog, so that it may have its natural growth, and you will notice that the frog will enlarge and resume its healthy and thriving condition, and crowd or pull the heel open to better advantage than any artificial theory for making horses' feet.—*By* S. STONE.

Against Spreading for Contraction.

Many writers advise the spreading of the foot at the time of shoeing.

This is a very old custom, but I have discarded it for nine years past, except in extreme cases. A foot can be spread very quickly by putting on a shoe and then opening it at the heels with the tongs, but this process generally gives pain to the horse, and this pain is constant night and day, for the animal cannot take off his shoes at night as a man can, when a pair of boots hurt his feet,

My method will not spread a foot as quickly as the old plan, but it is more effective in the end and does not entail the possibility of a permanent injury to the horse. It is as follows :

A shoe is made in summer without calks ; in winter with very low ones, just sufficient to prevent slipping. The heel is cut down quiet low so as to get all the frog pressure, and the foot is concaved a little at the heel, or from the heel nails back. The shoe should have the nail holes well toward the toe, and must fit the foot perfectly as far around as the heel nails, but from this point to the heels should project outside the shell. At the heels the shoe must be at each side from three-eighths to half an inch wider than the foot and convex from the heels as far forward as the last nails. In bad cases I do not drive more than six nails.

The shoe should be removed quite often, and must not be too convex or the foot will be spread too fast.

In this way of shoeing, when the horse is standing the feet will spread, and a circulation will be created inside the hoof, which will lead to the filling up of the cavity in the natural way, or in other words, to a permanent cure.

I have followed this plan for nine years and it never failed. Flat feet do not easily contract.—*By* H. V. D.

Shoeing Contracted Feet.

It is a fact known to all shoers who have made the anatomy of the horse's foot a study, that you cannot use a bar shoe in all cases of contraction. To illustrate : Let us take two different cases. First, we will take a foot that has a normal toe and outside quarter and heel, but the inside quarter and heel are contracted. Now, how can we use, in such a case, a bar shoe with a frog pressure ? I will give you my way of treating such a patient. First put the foot in an oil-meal poultice so that the poultice will come on the inside more than on any other part of the foot, for from twelve to thirty-six hours. After the foot has become soft use a shoe like that shown in Fig. 67. Fit the shoe to the foot. After the shoe is nailed on take a spreader (I use a

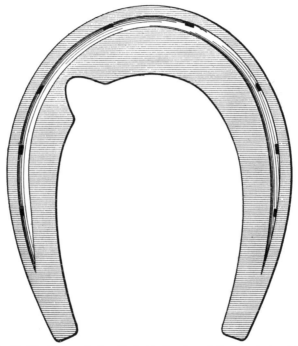

Fig. 67—The Shoe used when the inside Quarter and Heel are contracted

spreader in many cases of quarter crack and contraction), insert the spreader at the heels of the shoe and thus throw out the inside web of the shoe, for you will see that the shoe is weakened at the inside toe and will not give at any other point. It is unsafe to spread more than a little at a time.   I have shod a great number of feet in this condition and always with the best results, while a bar shoe could not have been used to advantage.

Now let us take another foot with both heels contracted. To look at it hastily it would suggest a bar shoe at once,

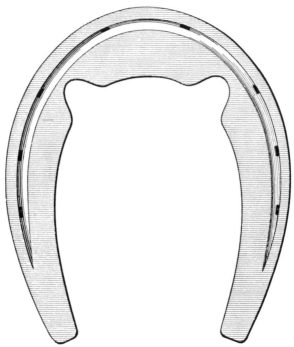

Fig. 68—Shoe used when both Heels are contracted.

but on more careful examination we find the foot hard and the frog as hard as a chip and almost crowded out of existence.   Now let us see if a bar shoe would be the best for this foot.   We think not, for, if we apply the bar shoe and get a direct frog pressure, the pressure on the internal or sensitive frog, will in most cases be too severe and cause more inflammation than existed before, and we will have aggravated the trouble instead of curing it. In this case my treatment would be similar to the first case in many respects.

I first level the foot, but lower the toe as much as I can with safety. Then I take a small saw and saw the foot open at both heels till I get through and start the blood, I then put on the shoe shown in Fig. 68, and spread as before.

Shoeing in this way, as your patients are driven up to your shop, you can take your compasses and spreader, slip out and expand the foot by spreading the shoe without removing it from the foot.—*By* H. M. S.

Contracted and Hoof-bound Feet.

Contraction of the feet is a disease more frequent among horses than any other to which they are subject, and it affects road and draught horses alike. It results from the hoof losing its moisture and thus becoming hard and feverish. Horses raised on farms always suffer from this disease. The causes are hard, dry floors and a lack of frog pressure. Its distinguishing features are a long, narrow foot, as shown in Fig. 69 of the accompanying engravings, and a large, high coronet as seen in Fig 70.

If contracted at the quarters there is a strong wall at the heel and toe, as illustrated in Fig. 69, but if contracted at the heels the wall is strong everywhere excepting at the heels.

The best remedy is the bar shoe, with nail holes around the toe. The wall should be raised, especially at the heels, until a frog pressure is obtained. The sole should be pared but slightly, because a thick sole acts as a brace and prevents the foot from shrinking. The shoe must bear on the frog and the feet should be soaked in water every night.

There are other methods of shoeing that might be adopt-

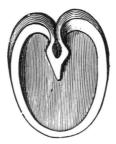

Fig. 69—Showing a Foot Contracted at the Quarters as described by " F. G."

ed in cases where there is no lameness. For instance : The foot can be pared as in the first method and then shod with plain shoes drawn down at the heel or with a tip

Fig. 70—Showing the prominence of the Coronet in a Contracted Foot.

around the toe. This tip requires about six nails, and allows the tip to bear on the ground. The horse should stand on a dirt floor and wet cloths must be wrapped around the foot every night for at least a month. The shoeing should be repeated every fourth week. It will be observed that in the center of the frog is a point called the V, which in a contracted foot is very hard and sharp. Now when the frog is pressed on the ground this V penetrates the foot and forces it open just as a wedge would. The country horse has broad, flat heels and hardly any V to enter the frog. In some cases the horse may be lame for some time after shoeing, but by keeping the feet moist a cure will be affected.

It must be remembered that the wall is the weakest near-

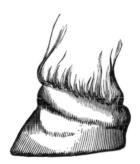

Fig. 71—Showing a Hoof-Bound Foot.

est the heel, and at the frog nearest the coronet. Contracted feet have, of course, hard, long and narrow frogs, which are generally affected with a disease called thrush or frog-rot. This is, however, easily cured by applying salt and turpentine every two or three days or a week or so—unless it breaks out above the hair, and then it is a case for the veterinary surgeon.

Hoof-bound feet are distinguished by a ridge running completely around the hoof, as shown in Fig. 71. The disease resembles contraction, except that the coronet is not enlarged. It is first perceived at the hair and grows downward, being at its worst when about one-third of the way down. It is found only on front feet and generally only on those of horses raised on hard soils. It completely cripples the horse, making him unfit for any use for at least a month, or until the wall of the foot becomes soft and pliable.

In shoeing in such cases the sole should be pared until it responds to the pressure of the thumb, and the outside of the wall must be rasped away considerably. But, of course,

Fig. 72—Showing a Foot shod with Tip, and with the Frog bearing on the ground.

judgment must be employed according to the circumstances attending each case. Put on a plain bar shoe that bears equally on the frog, toe, heel and quarters—in other words a perfect level bearing. The rest depends on the hostler. The feet should be soaked every evening in blood-warm water for about twenty minutes, and then wrapped in wet cloths for the night. The animal must stand only on a clay floor. It is necessary for the ridge to grow out as the foot grows downward, and for this six to eight months are required.

I have seen cases of this disease in horses fresh from the country and in animals which have never been shod. The treatment that I have advised will insure a noticeable improvement in from four to six weeks. Fig. 72 represents a foot shod with a tip, and with quarter, heel and frog bearing on the ground.—*By* F. G.

Favors Spreading for Contraction.

My method of treating tender or contracted feet is as follows : As soon as the frost is out of the ground remove the winter shoe and pare the foot all it will bear, especially at the heel. Scrape and cut the horn from the sole around the frog, and press on the sole with the thumb until it gives under the pressure. The braces must never be cut very much, and the frog should not be cut at all. A flat shoe with a very low toe calk and no heel calks is then put on and the insides of the heels are clipped nearly to a point. Make the shoe to cover the foot well, never use a short shoe and have the nail holes slant inwards.

Don't hew the foot down to fit the shoe, but always make the shoe to suit the foot. At the heel the shoe should be $\frac{3}{4}$ of an inch wider than the foot. From the point of the frog to the heel (inside) the shoe should have an advantage of $\frac{3}{16}$ of an inch in height. To measure this correctly apply a straightedge or square to the bottom of the shoe. Then, with the aid of a pair of tongs and a helper, spread the foot out to the full width of the shoe at the heel and keep it there until the nails are in at the heel. Use small nails and do not draw too tight. The object is to bring the frog on the ground. With superfluous horn, etc., all removed and a shoe fitted concave, as I have described, the frog will flatten and the foot expand rapidly.

For draft horses use a very low heel calk, and when the ground is frozen use the common shoe with clips. Do not employ a rasp to file under clinches, because this cuts across the grain of the hoof and injures it. I use a very small gouge, the width of a nail, and take out a little under the nail. This will give a good clinch every time. For light driving horses the nails should be driven hard and well clinched and clipped close with the clinch-cutter, then filed down and smoothed.—*By* S. C. C.

Contracted Feet.

I will give my mode of spreading a contracted foot. The tool I use for the purpose is illustrated in the engraving Fig. 73. It is about 8 inches long, the jaws are $\frac{7}{16}$ or $\frac{1}{2}$ inch thick, and the screw is about $3\frac{1}{2}$ inches long. It is put on the foot with the short side hooks (which are about $\frac{1}{4}$ inch

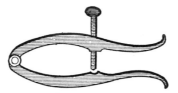

Fig. 73—Tool used for Spreading Contracted Feet.

long) in the heel. You can spread the heel just as much as it will bear. Fit the shoe considerably wider than the foot was before the heel was spread, level the shoe from the last nail hole out so that it will tend to give outward instead of inward as the weight comes on it. A little practice will teach the smith how much the foot will stand,

and how large the shoe should be, then lay the spreader flat on the foot, with the side hooks in the heel, and turn the screw. The larger the thread is on the screw the easier it will be to spread the foot. A good smith can tell whether the heel or toe is too long by looking at the foot.— *By* B. B.

Shoe for Contracted Feet.

Contraction is caused by the feet becoming hard from neglect in not being taken care of. The shoer drives the shoe on without properly preparing the foot. The quarters turn in and draw together at the heel, and the horse, as a consequence, becomes lame and cannot travel. What is the remedy for this defect? Some farriers claim that the horse

Fig. 74—Shoe for Contracted Feet.

should be turned out in marshy ground until the hoof becomes softened, when the difficulty will disappear. This plan is generally impracticable, as the owner of the horse wants to use him.

Others say the shoe should be made wide and nailed on while the hoof is spread with a pair of tongs. Still others use wide shoes and pretend to believe that contractions can be cured by them. Many other methods have come under my observation, and none of them are of much if any value.

My plan is to make a shoe expressly for contracted feet and the sketch, Fig. 74, will illustrate my idea. The dotted line, *A*, represents a joint made by simply cutting a common shoe through the center of the toe with a half round chisel. Holes, as shown, are then punched in each part of the severed shoe near the proposed joint, and countersunk on the inner surface. The toe calk, *B*, is then made, holes being punched in it and countersunk to correspond with the holes in the shoe. The parts are then riveted together as shown in the cut. The concavity of one part of the shoe fitting the convexity of the other, a perfect hinge is formed which can play beneath the toe plate or calk *B*. Care should be taken not to have the two surfaces fit too tightly. They must be loose enough to move easily upon each other. Then the heels of the shoe are turned up, not too high, but so as to bring them on a level with the toe and drawn outward so as to stand well apart. They should round outward, so that when the horse's weight comes upon them they will spring slightly apart. Small clips should be turned up on the inner edge of the shoe just in front of the heels, as shown at *D, D,* to catch inside of the quarter and hold the foot apart while it is being spread by the animal's weight upon the shoe. If the shoe is made as described you will have no difficulty in spreading the foot and curing the worst case of contraction.—*By* A. S.

Contracted Feet—Against Hot Fitting.

Permit me to say a few words in regard to shoeing contracted feet. It is cruel for a man to nail iron to the foot of a horse and then spread it with tongs or anything else. A good shoer can spread the hoof enough by driving the nails, by leaving the shoes full wide and setting the nail close against the inside of the nail-hole of the shoe each time he puts one on. The best way to use a contracted foot is *not to shoe it at all.* No man ever saw a contracted foot on a horse that was never shod, nor ever will he.

The frog of the foot of the horse should never have a knife or anything touch it in shoeing, nor should a shoe that takes the frog off of the ground ever be nailed on a foot. The frog is the life of the foot, and it is the wedge that holds the heels apart and causes the hoof to expand.

The injudicious method of paring away the frog and sole prevents the bars from touching the ground. The sensible plan is, first, to let the frog and sole acquire their natural thickness. Second, lead the horse to a gravel meadow, stuff the hollow of the foot with cow-dung or tar ointment, and leave him in the meadow, renewing the dung or ointment every day.

Applications of oils and brutal spreading of the feet with tongs never cured a contracted foot.

I will also say that a smith who is unable to fit a shoe to a foot without burning it level should be driven out of the trade. Burning a foot makes the hoof so hard that a knife cannot cut it when it gets cold, and the foot must necessarily be ruined sooner or later.—*By* M. T.

Contracted Feet.

My plan for treating a hoof-bound foot is to first pare the toe close but leave all I can across the quarters, and then fit the shoe nicely and put it on, driving the nails in the best part of the foot. Six nails will do. I then take the rasp and file off the front of the foot round but flat for a space of

3 to 3½ inches wide, and extending about two-thirds of the way up the foot. The center of this space should be filed the most. The object of this is to take away the strength from the front of the foot, for it is the pressure coming from the front which cramps or contracts the heel.—*By* J. H.

Quarter Cracks and Contracted Feet.

On the subject of quarter cracks and contracted feet, I will say that I use Prof. Magner's expansive shoe or a common, thin-heeled shoe or tip, which allows the heel and frog to come in contact with the ground. Either of these shoes will cure a quarter crack where a bar shoe fails to do so, and they are also the best shoes for contracted feet. I

Fig. 75—Showing the Shoe used by "Vulcan" for Contracted Feet.

would also advise, at the same time, the application of a mild blister around the coronet, not to draw a blister but simply to stimulate and cause growth. Use also veterinary vaseline or any other hoof ointment. Pare the foot as you would any common foot. If Magner's shoe is used the spreader should be employed three times a week and each time the shoe should be spread about $\frac{1}{16}$ of an inch. The shoe and spreaders are shown in the illustration herewith. Fig 75 represents the shoe, Fig. 76 the spreaders, and Fig. 77 shows the spreader C and B applied to the shoe A.

To make the shoe, select and ordinary hand-made shoe, then take a piece of Norway iron $\frac{3}{4} \times \frac{3}{8}$, chamfer the end, then weld on the inside edge of the shoe, cut it off and chamfer to an edge. It should project below the bearing surface of the shoe from $\frac{5}{8}$ to $\frac{3}{4}$ of an inch. Then drill a $\frac{3}{8}$

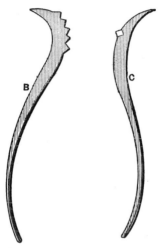

Fig. 76—Showing the Spreaders.

hole in each side between the second and third nail holes and file into them to weaken the shoe so that it will spread easily. When fitted, the spurs on the wheels should fit into the commissures between the frog and bars. After the shoe is fitted, if the ends of the spurs press on the sole, file them off a little.

For a quarter crack there need be but one spur and one hole drilled. They must be on the same side as the quarter crack and that is generally the inside. My theory is that quarter crack is caused by the shell growing too small for

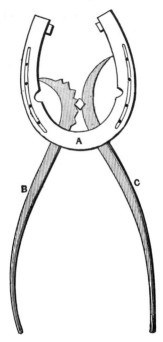

Fig. 77– Showing the Spreader applied to the Shoe.

the bones within it. When you remove the pressure you cure the quarter crack.—*By* VULCAN.

Contracted Feet and Quarter Crack.

Almost every horseshoer has his own ideas with regard to doing certain kinds of work, and very often different shoers will accomplish the same end by very dissimilar means. For instance, in cutting down a hoof some cut the toe well down and take nothing from the heel, while others cut down both. For contracted feet some shoers use a shoe very wide at the heel, reasoning that the hoof will follow the shoe, while others believe that such a shoe has a tendency to contract the feet.

I think there are general principles that ought to govern all shoers. I do not claim to have gone to the bottom of the matter, but I can give a few points that will at least be useful to beginners. In treating a case of contracted foot, I first remove the old shoe by carefully cutting all the clinches, and if possible remove each nail separately. I

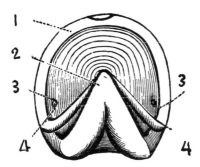

Fig. 78—Bottom View of a Horse's Foot. Showing the Seat of Corns.

then pare the hoof down to as near the natural form as possible. A hoof is never pared enough if any dead matter is left inside.

One of the most important points in shoeing is to never allow a shoe to remain on the foot too long. While a shoe is on, the foot is prevented from wearing, the waste matter remains and in time will spoil the foot by rotting some of the essential parts, frog, braces, etc., and corns will be caused by the direct pressure from the bottom or by the side pressure from the spoiling of the braces or bars.

Be sure that you never cut the braces lower than the outer horn, and always make the seat of a corn lower than either.

If the heel is contracted, and you have left the braces full, then make the shoe somewhat convex at the heel and let it curve directly under the heel of the foot —not outside, for that has a tendency to push the heel in. Leave it so that when it is nailed on, the hoof and shoe do not meet at the heel. There must be a space of one-eighth to three-sixteenths of an inch left there. Be careful not to burn the hoof, for that is very injurious, and be sure to make the shoe fit the horn of the hoof nicely. The outside hard part I call horn is what nature intended the horse to travel on, with perhaps some assistance from the frog. The shoe should bear evenly, and the nails used should not be too large.

The cure for interfering is to make the inside of the shoe the highest. For extreme cases, behind, I make the inside of my shoe nearly straight and very short; the toe calk is about one-third the distance around the shoe from the inside heel, the outside of the shoe follows the horn well round, and the toe calk is very short. Where there is only a slight tendency to interfere, it will only be necessary to keep the toe a little around toward the inside, and perhaps a little the highest on the inside ; it is not a good plan to turn the inside heel in too much, for horses do not strike with it. Shoe in the same way for fore feet except in making the inside web much heavier than the outside. I see most shoers take particular pains to make the outside of the hoof look very smooth and nice regardless of the harm so done. They rasp off nature's covering well up to the hair, which is a great injury to the hoof.

Some have called the outside the skin of the hoof, which I think is very proper. I advise being very careful not to disturb the outside more than is strictly necessary.

I generally put on over the crack a thin plate of iron held to place with about six screws, which enter the horn about one-fourth of an inch. I weld on a calk in front of the crack, do not let the shoe bear back of it, and generally cover over with tar to keep out the dirt. A crack extending up the toe of the hoof clear through the horn and up to the hair is rather a serious matter, and requires careful treatment by a man who understands his business.

Let me say again, do not cut away the frog. It is a cushion formed to give the horse ease on hard roads, and perhaps it also supplies the hoof with moisture. In the engraving annexed, Fig. 78, may be seen the various parts of the foot to which I have alluded : 1 is the horn ; 2, the frog ; 3, the seat of corns, and 4 4 are the braces.

Contraction—Interfering.

I will give you in brief my experience in shoeing contracted feet. I shall not lay down any particular theory by which to shoe all horses, for I do not believe that all horses can be shod alike with good success. Flat feet do not generally contract, but the reverse.

Now, with regard to shoeing, the smith must use good judgment in preparing the foot to be shod. Some feet naturally want more paring than others. My method is to fit the feet as nearly natural as possible. Make the shoe level nearly two-thirds the way round, and convex the heels, commencing at or near the back nail hole of the common shoe, but do not punch the nail holes so far back as the common shoe, and only drive six nails in a shoe. The shoes should be removed once in three or four weeks, according as the hoof spreads. Do not convex the shoe too much or you may cause quarter cracks. Let the shoe bear all around on the shell, but lightly on the heels, and fit the shoe quite wide for a foundation to spread upon. I have practised this way for the last eight or ten years, and have never known a case to fail if the owners followed my instructions in taking care of the horses.— *By* H. V. DUDLEY.

Contracted Feet—Poulticing.

In my practice as horseshoer I have found that in many cases, if not a majority, contraction is the cause of stumbling, overreaching, interfering, etc. We can shoe and help matters, but if we will at the same time soften and expand the foot we can effect a permanent cure, for when the foot is contracted, no treatment will cure the muscles that move the leg, because contraction of the foot is nearly always accompanied by wasting of the muscles of the breast, arm and shoulder, thereby bringing about an unnatural action.

Stand in front of the horse, and notice the quarters of the hoof; if they incline downward and inward, the hoof is contracted. The natural warmth of the hoof is the same as the air, and if the foot is warmer, it is not healthy. If the horse is lame, you will find the foot hard; pull off the shoe and let the owner soak the animal's feet in flaxseed meal, made with boiling water like mush. Put in this poultice a little sal soda and let the feet remain poulticed twenty-four hours. If the horse must be shod first, before the poultice is applied, pull off the shoes, examine the feet to see if there are any corns; if there are none and there is a large amount of hoof, remove some of it, so that the slope of the hoof is like the slope of the fetlock. Should the heels be low do not make them any lower; open them up, but not enough to bring the blood, weaken the hoof a little between the bars and the point of the frog, and open deeply backward into the fissures of the frog ; open the central frog fissure a little, from base to point, the object being to cause expansion to take place through the center of the hoof.

Now for the shoe ; the best is a common convex shoe, with even bearing alike on wall and sole, extending one-half over the hoof. The outside of the shoe should extend no farther out than the wall. Bevel the heels of the shoe next to the wall outward from the heel nail hole out. Don't have a short shoe, but let it be long, and remember that most stable floors slant backward, and an elevation of the heels will make the horse stand more at ease. When the shoe is ready nail it on the foot with as small nails as possible. Don't draw up very tight, nor pare the sole. Use the poultice night and day if possible, and if in a short time the horse is not better, take off the shoe and examine to see where the trouble lies. Don't permit the owner of the horse to keep the shoes on more than four weeks, and a less time would be better.

This is the way I treat contracted feet, and I have good success. Try it and you will find it makes a vast difference in the travel of the horse.—*By* RAB.

Contracted Feet Should be Kept Moist.

I will now give you my plan for shoeing a horse with contracted feet. If the feet are badly contracted I pare the soles very thin to make the feet spread easily, and fit the shoes beveled toward the outside edge from the last nail hole to the end of the heel. Before the shoe is nailed on, a small sponge is placed on the sole and covered with a piece of leather, which is nailed on with the shoe. Several small holes may be made in the leather for the admission of moisture.

It is of great importance to keep the feet moist, so that

the frog will keep out the heels when they spread. If the feet are but slightly contracted the soles need not be pared, and the leather and sponge may be omitted. I do not like the idea of standing a horse in water that reaches to his ankles, for excessive moisture makes the hoof brittle. All that is necessary is to keep the sole and frog cool and soft, and this object can be attained with a packing of sponges, moss or felt.—*By* HIGHLAND.

Clipped Shoe for Contracted Feet.

Concerning the shoeing of contracted feet, I think the shoe should be clipped on the inside of the heel in order to

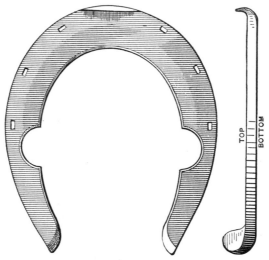

Fig. 79—Shoeing Contracted Feet, as done by C. W. Kohler.

weaken it back of the last nail as shown in the accompanying illustration, Fig. 79. The spreader is intended to spread the heel only and not to tear the wall of the foot from the sole. The main point is to keep the foot as short as possible.

I have shod horses in this way and secured a good open heel in about three months. In one of these cases the horse had been shod with the Roberge spring without being benefited at all.

Where one heel only is contracted I use Prof. Rich's half-bar shoe* and find it very efficacious, for there is generally some of the frog left in such a foot.—*By* CHAS. W. KOHLER.

Form of Shoe for Contracted Feet.

My way of shoeing contracted feet is as follows :

Pare the sole of the foot so that it can be sprung with the thumb, then fit on a medium weight shoe, without calks, and make a clip as shown in the accompanying illustration,

Fig. 80—Showing " F. E. B.'s" Method of Shoeing Contracted Feet.

Fig. 80, on the inside of each heel, to set inside of the bars on each side of the frog ; then set the shoe and spread the heel a little at a time. The foot must spread and the clip takes the strain off the nails and spreads the foot at the heels, where it should be spread.—*By* F. E. B.

---

* See " Artistic Horseshoeing " by Prof. Geo. E. Rich, published by M. T. Richardson, New York.

Improved Shoe for Contracted Feet.

Various ideas are set forth as a preventive and a remedy for contraction. Nearly every one who thinks that he knows anything about the disease at all has some peculiar notion of his own as to how and in what manner it should be treated.

I will not enter upon the subject to a very great ex-

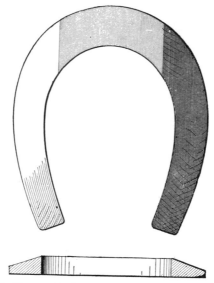

Fig. 81—Shoe used by Isaac A. Cavanagh for Contracted Feet.

tent, nor touch upon the many theories that are advanced for the relief or permanent cure of the trouble. Neither will I consider the causes that bring on the disease, nor prescribe any new expedient for a permanent cure. I will simply set forth a mode of proceeding that in every ordinary case will be sure to give satisfactory results.

Suppose, then, that a horse having a contracted foot is brought to a shop to be shod. Say that he is a work horse. The owner, we will say, is a poor man, who wants to work him if he can walk at all. He cannot afford to have his horse laid off for three or four weeks or more, and undergo a regular course of veterinary treatment. Under these circumstances, then, I would advise the following treatment:

Examine the foot well, and if the heels have grown high and present a squeezed, tight-looking appearance, with the entire surface of the sole and frog extremely hard and bonelike, the first thing you should do is to rasp or pare down the heels and soles, so as to relieve the foot from this unnatural iron-clad compressure, if I may use the expression. Do not pare the sole too thin; pare so that it will yield under strong pressure from your thumbs. Open out the heels in good shape, but do not pare between the frog and the bars; keep that part solid and strong, but loosen every other part of the foot as much as you can without injury to the sole.

The practical shoer will understand the sort of paring I mean better than any words of mine can convey to him. Now, having the foot ready, you can prepare the shoe somewhat as follows:

Any ordinary shoe will do, providing it has a moderately wide web; keep the nails well forward in the shoe, so that the foot will have every chance to spread. If it be a factory shoe, probably you need not put any nails in the back holes, particularly if the foot be short, which is seldom the case in contraction. Bevel the shoe on the outside of both webs, on the foot surface, commencing at a point about two inches from the center of the toe, and gradually beveling off to the ends of the heels. Towards the heels the shoe should have a good sloping bevel. The accompanying illustration,

Fig. 81, shows how the foot surface of the shoe should look, and also the shape of the heels.

Fit the shoe well to the foot, making sure that it has an even and level bearing all around. If the job be well and neatly done, you will find that in the first shoeing the foot has improved. Use this kind of a shoe for two or three

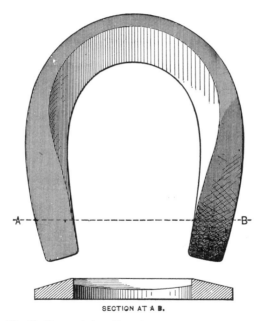

SECTION AT A B.

Fig. 82—Shoe made by "M. J. S. N." for Contracted Feet.

shoeings, in the meantime using some good foot ointment or preparation to soften and stimulate the growth of the foot. If you do this, take my word for it, all will go well, and the owner will not lose money by being obliged to lay the horse off for treatment.—*By* ISAAC A. CAVANAGH.

A Shoe for Contracted Feet.

The accompanying illustration, Fig. 82, represents a horseshoe used by some smiths for spreading the heels of hoof-bound or contracted feet. The outside is beveled off so that when the weight comes on the foot it will tend to spread the hoof. The nail holes are made well forward, so as to allow the back or heel more room to expand. It will readily be seen that with a shoe so formed the pressure on the hoof will be considerable every time the horse makes a step.—*By* M. J. S. N.

Shoeing a Mule's Contracted Foot.

A man came to my shop once with a lame mule. The animal's feet were so contracted that he could hardly walk. A German veterinary surgeon came with the owner of the

Fig. 83—Showing the Piece welded on the under side of the Heel for Contraction.

mule and under this surgeon's instructions I did the shoeing as follows:

I first made a shoe, using for the job a Burden's No. 2

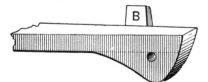

Fig. 84—Showing the Piece welded on the Inside.

hind-shoe, and next welded a piece about 2 inches long on the under side of the heel on each side, as shown at *A*,

in Fig. 83 of the accompanying engravings ; then a hole
was drilled through each side, $\frac{9}{32}$-inch in diameter, and a
piece welded upon the inside and allowed to stick up half an
inch from the top of the shoe as shown in Fig. 84, at B. I
next made a $\frac{3}{8}$-inch round rod, long enough to reach across
the shoe, and drew out each end small enough to enter the

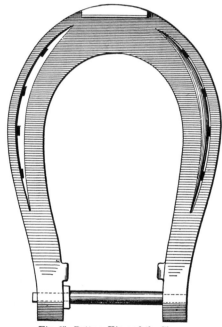

Fig. 85—Bottom View of the Shoe.

holes drilled. A shoulder was left for the shoe to rest
against. One of the ends was made long enough for an
extra nut, as shown in Fig. 85. Then after cutting a thread
upon the longest end up to the sholder, I opened or spread
the shoe and screwed a nut down to the shoulder.

I next put one end of the little cross-bar into the shoe and then inserted the other end, and narrowed up the shoe, bringing it up tight to the shoulders. I leveled the foot, then took a $\frac{1}{4}$-inch wood chisel and cut just inside of the heel braces to allow the entrance of the pieces marked B, in Fig. 84.

When everything was fitted nicely I nailed the shoes on the two front feet (which were the contracted ones), and then took a little wrench and spread the hoofs by screwing up the nut upon the spreading-bar. The piece B took the strain from the nails : with an ordinary shoe, nails could not have been driven far enough back to spread the heels as did the piece B.

The owner was told to give the bar a quarter turn around every day. The threads cut upon the cross-bar were 20 to the inch. In Fig. 85, a bottom view of the shoe is given. The mule had not been able to work for two years, but he is now cured. The surgeon gave the following prescription for a dressing—this was applied every day by pressing it into and around the frog and top of the hoof—Kosmalein, 4 ounces ; ammonia, 2 ounces ; carbolic acid, 20 drops ; new linseed oil, 1 pint.—*By* C. M. LYON.

White Pine Pitch for Contracted Feet.

I had a horse that had contracted feet very badly. I used white pine pitch on them, and was surprised to see what a good effect it had. It softened the hoof and it began to grow, and I believe if I had kept it on all the spring he would have had a foot as big as an elephant. I covered the foot all over, with the pitch melted so as to stick well.—*By* H. A. S.

CHAPTER VI.

CORNS AND HOW TO TREAT THEM.

This difficulty though a prolific cause of trouble to all horseshoers has, for some reason or other, received less attention than its merits would seem to deserve. Such articles as have been contributed to the columns of the *Blacksmith and Wheelwright,* are presented in this chapter for the consideration of the reader.

Shoeing to Prevent Corns.

There have been many writers who have appeared to settle the question of the cause, prevention, and cure of corns, their theories being all based upon the assumption that vertical pressure causes the corn. Respectfully I ask that such writers go a little deeper into the subject and see if the facts do not point to transverse pressure as the cause, and to vertical pressure, rightly applied, as the preventive and cure, where cure is possible. Will the writer who advises paring out the sole and concaving the shoe so that the entire hoof contact shall be with the shell *only,* explain why it is necessary to prevent the sole from taking any part of the pressure as far as possible? Of course, the answer may be:

"Because sole pressure makes the corns, and removing sole pressure will cure them."

But, some of us don't accept this. We believe that all parts of the foot have functions to perform, and that removing vertical pressure by digging out the sole, concaving the shoe to the extent advocated by some, cutting away the hoof at the quarters, or springing the shoe off, instead of being curative is injurious, in that it aggravates the real difficulty—*i.e.*, transverse pressure caused by contraction, Nature's own cure for which is vertical pressure in a proper way with every step the horse takes, tending to expand the foot.

It is possible, of course, that there may be some hidden meaning, some mysterious knowledge not vouchsafed to ordinary mortals back of the statement of the smith who, as he fits the shoe to a slightly contracted hoof, the inner quarter slightly wired in, says: "I want to give all the room I can on that inner quarter."

What does he do? Spreads the heels of the shoe apart. Puts the narrowed, pinched heel between rather than squarely on top of the heels of the shoe, and the chances are that the top surface of the shoe at the heels upon which this slight bearing is made will be beveled inward. Perhaps there is a reason why a foot shod this way, "with a good, broad, open heel," as it is called, should find relief; but there are those who don't see it, and such contend that the hoof should rest upon a level surface, and that the heels of the shoes should be kept in where all of the back part of the hoof which would bear upon a level surface shall be, *on* the shoe, *never between* to hold the foot from expanding at every step, as it inevitably would if it rested upon a level surface. There are those who advocate beveling the top of the shoe at the quarters and heels outward to increase the tendency to expand from vertical pressure. In moderation this may be, for some feet, a good thing, but to bevel them inward, as hundreds of them are, must put the horse to excruciating torment at every step. I have in mind a pair of forward shoes which were taken from a lame horse and replaced with a pair the top surfaces of which were made strictly level, or plain, by a straightedge, the result being that inside of a week the horse went perfectly sound and the shoer was looked upon by its owner as a most wonderful man. The old shoes have been kept, and it is my belief that the inside of the web at the heels is fully one-eighth of an inch lower than at the outside ! On such a shoe the foot was practically in a dish, to be pinched as by a vise at each step.—*By* S. W. GOODYEAR.

Corns in Horses' Feet.

What is a corn in a horse's foot, and what are the causes of it ? In attempting to answer this question 1 would say, in the first place, that misplaced blood produces the corn appearance, on the same principle as a bruise. The blood settles under the nail of a jammed finger. It is similar in a horse's foot. When the hoof grows down and the bottom of the foot has been cut off times enough to show the corn or red appearance, every one with common consent says the horse has corns. It is blood out of place which gives the corn or red color. The horse might have been lame months before the corn made its appearance on the bottom, in the angle between the crust of hoof and bar.

It is said that the cause of corns is bad shoeing, shoes badly fitted, short shoes, overmuch cutting away of the heel, etc., etc. Usually, I think, these hurts are the results of letting shoes stay on a longer time than they ought at one setting. The shoe goes forward with the growth of the foot, and the heel of the shoe drops off into the angle between the crust and the bar.

Fever in the foot for any cause, such as improper watering, feeding, sudden chills, an unusual drive, with improper care when released or stabled, in fact, from anything that interferes with the natural circulation of the blood in the foot or that cuts off the circulation in the vicinity of the germ of the corn, which is at the wing or widest point of the paddle bone, may be a cause of this difficulty. Thus, when the hoof has contracted for any cause, so that the shell of the foot rests on the bone, and has cut off the circulation, the result is similar to a bruise. It is misplaced blood, or a dead spot or a spot destitute of circulation, consequently it becomes sore and inflamed, and the hoof ceases to grow naturally. The red or corn appearance sometimes shows itself over various parts of the entire sole of the foot for similar reasons.—*By* S. S.

Cause and Treatment of Corns.

I think the owners of horses are, in a measure, to blame, but there may be cases where the shoer is at fault. Owners will not have shoes removed at the proper time, and the shoe, as a consequence, becomes bedded in the quarter or root of the corn. In such cases the shoer cannot be wholly to blame. I think the shoe should follow the shell of the foot, but not encroach upon the frog, nor bear more than equally on the heel. If left wide at the heel, contraction is apt to result.

In treating corns I have had good results by using butter of antimony—five drops at an application. Two applications will generally effect a cure in bad cases.—*By* G. H. De L.

Shoeing to Cure Corns.

A very good way to shoe a horse that has corns is as follows: Weld a toe calk lengthwise on the heel of the shoe, set the toe on the inside of the shoe, or on the inside edges, and cutting out of a rubber boot leg a piece the same size as the shoe, put it under the shoe.—*By* A. C. A.

Shoeing for Corns.

My way of curing horses that have corns, or are hoof-bound as we commonly call it, is as follows :

I use a common factory-made shoe that is not too light, the weight being made to depend upon the weight of the horse. The shoe has a toe and heel that are the same as those on the ordinary shoe, but I am careful not to have the toe too high, and I spring the heel away from the hoof behind at least one-fourth of an inch just behind the last nail, which should not be too close to the heel. That will expand the hoof half an inch or more in less than a year and the corn will disappear. When a quick cure is needed I cut the corn out well and burn black with a hot iron.—*By* A. B.

CHAPTER VII.

INTERFERING AND OVER-REACHING.

It will be observed by a careful perusal of this chapter that the methods of different shoers differ considerably. As in each case recited, the shoer has presumably met with more or less success with the plan suggested, it seems the duty of the editor to present the various methods described, and permit shoers to select such as seem to fit the particular case they may have to treat.

How to Shoe Interfering Horses.

The subject of interfering engrosses the attention of horse-shoers and those who use horses, to a greater extent than anyone unacquainted with the subject would suppose.

This defect in a valuable horse is of serious moment to those who value speed or require it in their business. It is said by many that the real cause of interfering is weakness in the limbs. There are cases where this cause is probably the correct one, and many others where it cannot be entertained at all. Interfering is a great misfortune to a horse, and to be remedied, requires strict observation and a practical understanding of the movements of horses' limbs. Horses that interfere front and behind, and also forge, require from the smith the exercise of considerable patience and judgment in the choice of a method of shoeing, which will give the most satisfactory results.

In shoeing the hind feet some weight the shoe, the outer half being wider than the inner. Others cut away the outside of the hoof, thus causing the foot to lean out and throwing the fetlock joint into an angular position, the shoe being level. This device produces an unnatural gait, and is a continual punishment to the animal as long as the angularity lasts.

Bare-footed horses seldom interfere, and when they do so, it is caused by carelessness on the part of those who

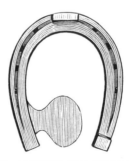

Fig. 86—A Half Bar Shoe for Interfering.

care for them, in not having the superfluous hoof removed by the rasp. A horse that has his hoofs pared level and the shoe also level, with the inner part of the shoe having a slightly greater radius than the outer part, with two nails just inside the toe, or none at all in severe cases, the shoe to be set under well and a clip put on the outside between the toe and quarter, will often give good results.

Projecting nails cause cutting in nine cases where the shoe does in one. For a horse that is almost incurable in striking, a half-bar shoe, made as shown in accompa-

nying illustration, Fig. 86, will be found very serviceable.
A half-bar shoe is one with a plate extending from the
inner half of the shoe resting on the frog. This allows
more area for the weight to rest on, and removes it from
the sole of the foot. Some horses never strike below a
six-mile gait, but between that and eleven-mile gait there
is often some fearful striking.

Speed horses should never be shod heavy behind. A
horse can pick his limbs up better when not burdened
with metal. The cords of the legs can be controlled better when taxed to give momentum to a weight of iron
not required.

The setting in of the shoe can also be observed when
the horse strikes with the front feet. Reduce the size of
the foot by cutting away the toe as much as possible.
Let the angularity commence at the heel, and relieve the
toe of as much hoof as the circumstances allow. This is
an advantage, as the hoof is reduced in size and brought
outside the line of danger in traveling. And this is all
that is required.

When a shoe begins to bend it has passed its point of
usefulness, and should be removed at the earliest oppor-
tunity. A warping shoe is most injurious to a horse's
foot. Many horsemen never think of tracing the ailments of their horses' feet to warping shoes ; but they
are an incessant source of danger. It often takes weeks'
time and loss of service to eradicate evils which they
produce.—*By* C. S.

Bad Case of Interfering Cured.

An otherwise valuable horse was an incorrigible inter-
ferer forward. He struck all the way from the ankle to
the knees, according to the speed at which he was driven,

and had to be booted anew often, for he literally wore his boots out in a short time. All the smiths in town who believed they could stop him had tried and failed.

A shoer from out of town having heard of the horse while on a visit, said he would like to shoe him, and was invited by a local shoer to use his shop and tools for the purpose. Turning a pair of shoes, removing the old ones, paring the feet, doing all the work of setting and finishing off the feet himself, in a self-reliant and handy way, in a strange shop, showed the man to be a workman.

The shoes were made with the web on the outside very much heavier and wider than on the inside. They were an exageration of the shape used by some of the best drivers of trotters to make a horse travel wider both forward and behind. A long, high side-calk was put on the inside web. There were no heel calks or toes put on. It seemed, to look at the awkward things, as though it would be a clear case of cruelty to animals to make horses wear them. The side-calk was more than an inch high.

"Won't it break his legs, or lame him to cant the feet over so much?" I asked. The answer was:

"If this horse is ever made to go without hitting, its got to be done by busting his gait. I think I can bust his gait with these shoes."

When the job was done, the horse was driven half a dozen miles or more. The roads were muddy, so that had he hit there would have been marks. Not a mark could be seen. Said the driver, "I have driven him up and down hill, and on level ground, from a walk to a 2:50 clip. It is the most wonderful thing I ever knew! If you had driven him the distance of a block before he would have hit a dozen times."

Said the shoer who had wrought the change, "I would

use a lower calk next time, and when his gait is thoroughly 'busted,' when he gives up his old way of going for good, he can be let down level."

This was one case; may there not be others like it? If among our score or more of shops this horse found no cure of his knocking until by chance an outsider took up the case, why is it not reasonable to suppose that there may be other places in which this wrinkle has been untried, but would be just the thing? Only for extreme cases would I advocate this plan.—*By* S. W. GOODYEAR.

Shoeing Interfering Horses.

I will give my plan for shoeing horses for interfering in front feet.

In the first place pare the foot perfectly level, then have your shoe the same thickness on both sides, but have the web of the outside of the shoe a little wider than the inside in order to have it some heavier on the outside. Then if the horse strikes with the inside quarter or between the quarter and toe of the foot, as is generally the case, begin straightening the shoe a little forward of the place that does the cutting. Make the inside of the shoe almost straight, leaving the inside heel as far away from the frog as possible, and have the inside of the shoe a little longer than the outside. Chamfer the shoe where it does the cutting from the upper and inner edge to the nail heads, and have the shoe fit in close enough at that point to let the hoof extend over the shoe about one-eighth of an inch and the round sharp edge with the rasp. After you have the shoe fitted be careful to set the toe directly opposite the point of the frog. I have had good success with several bad cases in this way.—*By* C. J. T.

The Cause of Interfering and its Remedy.

With regard to interfering horses my experience is that when the hoof is even, as in the case of a colt that has never been shod, there is never any interfering. By an even hoof 1 mean one on which, taking the frog from the center of the foot, I find about as much hoof inside the frog as outside of it. This perfectly level bearing of the feet inside and outside prevents all twisting or sidewise motions of the limbs while they are in motion. On the other hand, I find that in nine cases out of ten where two-thirds of the hoof is outside the frog the horses are knee-knockers and interferers. I think interfering is chiefly due to bad shoeing, that is by the smith taking a little more off the inside every time the horse is shod. This destroys the equal bearing and then the horse begins to interfere. To remedy it the hoof must be brought out on the inside and taken off on the outside.—*By* L. K.

Interfering.

With reference to interfering between horses' hind feet, I have employed the following method for over ten years, and it has given good satisfaction. I pare the outside of the foot the lowest and leave the inside the highest. I make my shoes the thickest on the inside and draw them as narrow as I can conveniently. I make the outside the thinnest, and of ordinary width. I fit the shoes as narrow from the toe to the heel of the inside as possible, so as not to get the nails too deep in the foot. I fit the outside the same as any other shoe.

My idea is to have the foot the highest on the inside, which throws the pastern joint out from the other foot when it is set on the ground and while the opposite foot passes it in making the step. I fit the shoe a little narrow on the inside and take care not to rasp the foot quite to the shoe, so that the shoe itself will not bo apt to strike. Considerable judgment is necessary to bo exercised upon the part of the smith to be successful in cases of this kind. Nothing short of experience will take him through. It should be remembered that sometimes a horse cuts with the heel ; other times it is with the toe, hence it is not always necessary to fit the shoe narrow at both toe and heel. It is well, however, to do so on the first trial.—*By* G. W. D.

A Cure for Interfering—A Calk Swage.

A few words on the subject of interfering may be of interest for the reason that it is a matter on which no two shoers

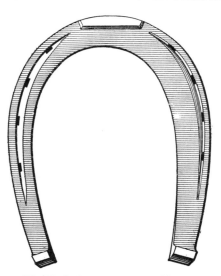

Fig. 87—A Shoe for Interfering Horses.

agree. What will cure one horse will often cause another to interfere. In ordinary cases paring the foot perfectly level, fitting the shoe very close and leaving out the heel nail on the inside, will effect a cure. The clinch from the heel nail working up often causes interfering. In bad cases I use a shoe like that shown in Fig. 87 of the accompanying illustrations. This shoe should be forged of the same thickness all around. I usually make the inside about one-half inch and the outside one inch in width, with a gradual taper in the toe. If this shoe is properly fitted to the foot it will stop the worst case of interfering. I am opposed to rocking, *i e.,* paring all on one side, as that is a direct cause of crooked and weak ankles. I admit that it will often prevent inter-

Fig. 88—A Swage for Calks.

fering, but the " remedy is worse than the disease." The useful little tool shown in Fig. 88 is a calk swage that I often find convenient in upsetting and squaring sharp calks and also in welding toe calks that have been partially loosened by sharpening. I think any explanation in regard to it unnecessary, as its construction is clearly shown in the cut.—*By* C. H. H.

A Shoe for Interfering Horses.

I will describe my way of shoeing interfering horses. Most smiths in shoeing an interfering horse, pare the foot on one side, a quarter or half an inch lower than on the other. Sometimes the paring is done on the inside and sometimes on the outside. Now, I was taught to pare the foot lower on the outside, taking out one-quarter of an inch so as to make the horse wide between the ankles.

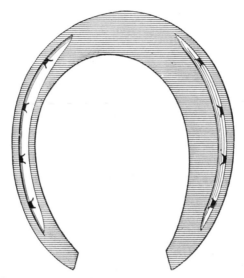

Fig. 89—A Shoe made by " J. J." for Interfering Horses.

I was told to make the shoe with about the same differ ence in height, the outside being about a quarter of an inch the lower. It is clear that by this method the horse's legs are strained all the time, and the bearing is all on the inside of the shoe, consequently the shoe will not remain on the foot long. My present method of shoeing is shown in the accompanying illustration, Fig. 89. The shoe is made wide on one side and of the same thickness, consequently when the horse stands upright on his feet there will be no strain, but when he puts up his foot to move, the wide or heavy side of the shoe, being on the inside, has a tendency to throw his feet or ankles apart.— *By* J. J.

Fitting Shoes, Curing Overreaching and Interfering.

I took two premiums in Indiana for horseshoeing, and therefore your readers may be interested in my methods of doing such work.

I first pare the hoof level, then fit the shoe to the hoof cold. If the horse is one that loses shoes easily, I drive the nails wedge shape, turning the points of the two toe nails toward the heel and the points of the heel nails to the toe. This makes a very strong job. If the horse interferes I rasp the outside of the hoof a very little lower than the inside and never turn the inside calk under the hoof as many smiths do to stop interfering.

For overreaching I pare the heel of the front hoof the lowest, and make the heel of the shoes thin and the toe thick. The hind shoe should have a thin toe and a thick heel, leaving the hoof high at the heel and turning the toe all it will bear. This will cure the worst cases. I think good nails are very essential to good shoeing. The main object of the smith should be to get the shoe fitted level and flat on the foot before the nails are driven. It will not answer to depend on the nails drawing the shoe to the hoof.—*By* J. C. D.

Shoeing to Prevent Interfering.

The majority of horses strike with the edge of the shoe or clinches, usually between the toe and heel nail. They do not strike with the heel calk, as a great many shoers think. It is only occasionally that a horse is found that strikes with the heel calk. Very few horses have a natural tendency to strike. The habit is usually brought on by careless driving. Over-driving, causing the horse to become leg weary, is a common cause of the difficulty. Allowing the shoes to remain on too long until the clinches work out, or the animal becomes smooth in the winter, or on icy roads, is also a cause. Some horses strike when they become poor or thin in flesh.

By attention to the sore ankles thus caused without changing the shoeing, they get entirely over the habit when they are again in good condition. The first thing, therefore, necessary to be done is to find out what particular part of the shoe the horse strikes with. My plan is to straighten out that part and clinch down smooth, rasping away the shell. If the horse is poor, I prescribe more feed and careful attention to the sore ankles. If he strikes from over-driving, I straighten a little and prescribe more careful handling. In the worst cases in winter time, I turn the outside heel calk, not the inside one, as some shoers recommend, in order to keep the foot from working in after it is placed on the ground. I shoe often enough to keep the horse from slipping. I think if these rules are intelligently followed by any shoer, he will have no difficulty with cases of this kind. It often requires two, and sometimes three, trials, especially if the horse has sore ankles, before a cure is effected. Some owners think that the smith should stop the worst cases and heal up the sore ankles by the first shoeing. This is unreasonable, as many readers will doubtless agree.—*By* F. H. S.

Interfering.

There are many ways to lessen, to some extent, the interfering of a horse, but what is applicable to one is not always good for another, and the more methods we are acquainted with the more likely we are to select one which will prove serviceable.

The following may be of advantage to some shoers :
Prepare the shoe as shown in Fig. 90, having no heel on

Fig. 90—Design for an Interfering Shoe with Side Calk.

the inside. Let the height of the iron answer for a heel,
the same as the ordinary style of interfering shoe. Have a

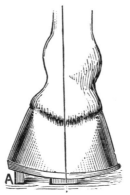

Fig. 91—Front View, Showing Calk on the Inside at *A* and the Angle of the Foot.

heel on the outside of the shoe. Weld a calk about one and
a quarter inches long back of the inside nail holes (as per

sketch at *A*) on the inside of the shoe. Bevel the toe calk off on the outside. Have the outside heel calk lower than the inside of the shoe. When done place the shoe on a

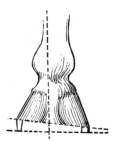

Fig. 92—Rear of Heels.

level surface and see that all the bearings touch. Heat and hot file the inside from the toe back as far as is required to an under level, and to within a little of the nail holes so as to remove all unnecessary projecting metal (for this pur-

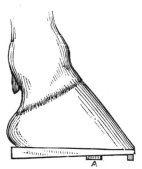

Fig. 93—Inside View of Hind Foot, Showing the Calk *A* and Toe Calk.

pose draw down the ends of a rasp, not fit for the floor, put two handles on it and you then have the best of double-handed files, with temper enough left in its center for all practical purposes). Leave the inside of the shoe, for some length, nearly straight if the horse is strong limbed, and leave the heels as wide as possible. This increases the area of bearing, but if the backing strap in going down hill draws his feet together it is essential that the inside heel should be quite thin and carried out of the line of danger, circumstances controlling in this point as in many others. Harden the *inside* of the toe calk and not the *outside*, thus retaining the level of the shoe as long as possible. Horseshoeing allows of no set method.—*By* C. S.

Interfering.

My method is, in the first place, to find what part of the hoof or the shoe comes in contact with the ankle. If the hoof does not show any mark, take a piece of chalk or a little tar and rub it on the ankle and start the horse. Let the horse be examined carefully until the smith has assured himself just what part of the hoof or shoe comes in contact with the ankle.. If a horse strikes with the toe at the first or second nail, straighten the shoe at that point and raise the inside calk a little so as to throw the ankle outward. If he strikes with the heel of the foot, straighten the shoe from the second toe nail back to the heel and take off the hoof at that point.

Some horses do not come in contact with the shoe ; it is the hoof that strikes. If a horse strikes with the heel calk turn it under a little. Apply the same methods with chalk or tar with the fore foot. If the horse interferes with the toe straighten that part of the shoe. If with the toe of the hoof at about the first or second nail where they are clinched, rasp the hoof away as much as it will bear, and lay in the clinches so as to be sure they will not work out, and raise the inside heel calks as much as may be deemed best.

If a horse's ankle stands in, or if his hoof appears as though the toe of the hoof was turned outward, raise the outside three-eighths of an inch higher than the opposite side. If in winter time let the inside calk be blunt and sharpen the outside. If the horse is heavy and well spread, weight the outside web twice as much as the inside.

If a horse strikes his knee, or is what we call a knee-knocker, the remedy to be applied is as follows: Fit up a common shoe letting the inside of the toe calk project over the shoe one-fourth or three-eighths of an inch. Let the outside of the calk be a little short so that the toe will wear on the outer corner. If the horse strikes below the knee the smith can take a heavier shoe and straighten it a little more than usual at the inside, back of the toe.—*By* J. I.

Interfering—Overreaching—Hot and Cold Fitting.

Probably there is no one thing there are so many theories about as the matter of horseshoeing. Now I want to say to all young men and new beginners, don't ever get a *pet* theory upon any subject. If you do, you will just as certainly fail as did the quack doctor who doctored an Englishman and cured him, and afterward doctored a Frenchman who had the same disease, and gave him the same treatment and he died. The doctor set it down in his memorandum book that what would cure an Englishman would kill a Frenchman. Now you may take two horses that interfere and shoe them just alike ; and you may cure the one and make the other worse, and the same is true of overreaching horses.

What is the cause? It is this: No two horses are exactly alike in any particular ; neither do they travel alike, or even stand still alike. In the matter of interfering the shoer must look his horse over and see him travel in order to arrive at anything like a correct idea of what is needed in his case.

For instance, a horse that hits forward, if he is a thick-breasted, well spread animal, generally needs a different kind of shoe from the thin horse, with both legs close together. If the shoer, or any one else, will stand in front or behind the thick, well-spread horse, when he is travel-ing, if he interferes, he will observe that when he lifts his feet it is done with a roll or swing inwards. That horse wants to be shod with a shoe of equal thickness all round but twice as wide on the outside, to weight the outside of the foot and make it balance.

If, however, your horse is thin, and his legs are close together, and he travels close, you want to make the shoe the thickest on the inside and straighten it a little in the spot where he hits. With the hind feet I have but little trouble. You should take particular notice how the horse stands and travels. If he carries his feet straight, pare the foot a little, the lowest on the outside, and set the shoe in a little on the inside, but if your horse toes out, as a great many do, set your shoe well round upon the inside toe and out at the heel, and trim off the outside toe, so as to make him travel square. These are general directions, and with me the treatment described has been successful in cases of interfering.

I have always found overreaching more difficult to over-come, but here again do not get any pet theory in your head. If I do not succeed the first time, I try some other method. Were I to shoe a horse that I had never seen before and knew nothing about, I should put heavy shoes in front and light ones behind; if this did not help the matter I would put on light ones all round.; or I would set the toe calk well back on the hind shoe and set the shoe nearly flush with the rim of the foot (no half-inch back for me); put

the heel calks of the front shoe one-half or three-quarters
of an inch from the heel, and bevel the heel from the ground
side to nearly a point. Horses generally outgrow this disagreeable habit as they grow older. I observe that one
shoer recommends using nothing but hind shoes. Now I
think that all wrong, for this reason : There are many
horses that have a very wide, flat foot ; if you use narrow
shoes there is nothing to protect the bottom of the foot,
and it is growing worse all the time ; but if you use a shoe
with a wide web it will take an equal part of the pressure
and keep the foot from sagging down.

I wish to say a few words about the much-talked-of subject, " Hot and Cold Fittings." I am for hot fitting in theory and cold in practice. But some one will say that is
inconsistent. My reason is, that while I do not believe a
shoe can be fitted to a horse's foot so nicely in any other
way as when hot, I usually fit cold to please my customers,
who know no more about a horse's foot than they do about
the internal arrangement of the kingdom of Heaven.
There seems to be considerable talk about what *is* hot and
cold fitting. I do not believe in heating a shoe white hot,
and burning the foot down without using the butteris or
knife, but I do believe in having the shoe moderately red.
Then place it on the foot and burn a little and pare a little
until you get the foot to the proper size and shape. Do not
have your shoe too cold, for if you do you may keep it on
so long as to heat the foot through and injure it.—*By*
GRANITE STATE.

Interfering, How to Prevent it.

In regard to interfering, I have had the best success with
horses that interfere by paring the foot as small as it will
do. Have the foot perfectly level, then fit the shoe to the

foot, not the foot to the shoe. Do not fit the inside of the shoe under the foot, and the outside full, but keep the inside of the shoe full and instead of putting a clip on the outside of the shoe put it on the inside of the shoe, about one-third the length of the shoe from the heel. I have found that this plan will stop the worst kind of cases of interfering if the ankles are not too badly swollen.—*By* G. F. J.

Curing an Interfering Horse.

Some time ago a young man came into my shop with a fine black filly tha was interfering badly, and asked me if I could cure her. Looking at the animal's legs I remarked

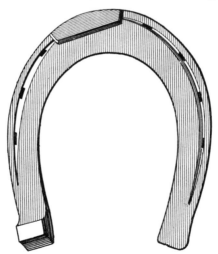

Fig. 94—A Shoe for Interfering Horses.

it was asking a good deal of a man to cure her in the condition she then was in. I believe I would be safe in saying that a circle of an inch and a half would not have covered the space on her legs that was raw and bleeding. But I informed him I would do the best I could, and I cured that mare. As my manner of treating such cases may be of benefit to some of my brother mechanics, I will describe it. I do not use a regular interfering shoe, for I find it will not work in a bad case of interference. Of course, I prepare the foot carefully, leaving the inside a little the higher, if possible. I then take any shoe and raising the heel calk on the inside, put my toe calk considerably past the center on the inside, leaving the outside calk plain, in other words without any calk, as shown in the illustration, Fig. 94. I have never known this mode of shoeing to fail in the very worst case.—*By* C. E. C.

Corns—Interfering—Overreaching — Welding Toe-Calks —Cold Fitting.

Nine persons out of ten will say that corns in horses' feet are caused by bad shoeing. My experience will justify me in saying that nine-tenths of the corns are caused by the owners of horses neglecting to get them shod as often as they ought. We are nearly all agreed that horses should be shod as often as once in every four to seven weeks, according to circumstances. Now, a great many horse owners, particularly farmers, will get a team shod, and, unless the horse becomes lame, will permit the shoes to remain on until they *grow off*.

If the horse has a round foot and the shoe was fitted close all around, in four or five weeks the shoe will have been carried forward by the growth of hoof, so that one or both of the heels will be off the wall, and in a short time corns will be produced. Now, if the owner would take his horse to the shop on some fixed date every month, instead of leaving the shoes on from seven to twenty weeks, horses would have fewer corns. In shoeing I prefer a wide heel and mule the heels of the forward shoes whether they have corns or not, on horses that have flat feet.

For interfering, level the foot and fit the shoe all around close. Then mule the inside heel slightly. In winter it is a good plan to turn the outside heel-calk, as it keeps the foot out of the trough of the road.

For overreaching I have the best success shoeing with long shoes all around. Let the heels of the forward shoes stick out an inch and the hind shoes three-quarters of an inch. As the forward foot raises the long shoe will raise enough so the hind foot will pass under, while with a short one the shoe will raise just enough for the hind shoe to hit the heels, causing a disagreeable clicking. I can do better and quicker work with knife and rasp than with butteris.

If the foot is grown out very long I take the cutting pliers and nip the hoof off from quarters to toe. This insures the removal of the stubs of nails, and with a sharp knife and rasp, the foot is soon ready. I practice cold fitting, although I do not think a thick shelled foot is injured by touching it with a red hot shoe that was previously fitted.

A thin-shelled foot I never press with a hot shoe. I was taught to weld toe-calks on shoes first and heel up afterwards, but I practice heeling shoes first and put on the toe-calk when ready to use the shoe. If you toe last there will be heat enough in the shoe after welding the calk to fit the shoe. I let the heels, which are nearly cold, drop on the wall of the foot and hold the toe, which is red hot, an inch away from the foot while fitting. After the shoe is fitted and level, harden the toe and nail on. I know a great many advocate heating a shoe red hot after the foot is prepared and the shoe fitted and press the foot for an instant with the hot shoe. But all the advantage they claim is an equal bearing and that the shoe will be less liable to come off.

Now I can with knife and rasp get as good a bearing, and with a good nail fasten the shoe so that it will stay longer than it ought.—*By* J. W. NICHOLS.

Shoeing for Interfering.

My way of shoeing a horse that interferes in front at the toe, is shown in the accompanying illustration, Fig. 95. I take a piece ⅜-inch steel and make a pair of shoes to fit the feet, making the outer side the heaviest in the web, but

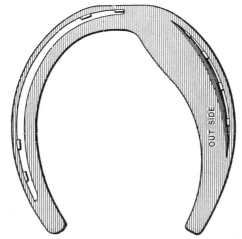

Fig. 95—A Shoe for Interfering Horses, as Made by " C. H. M."

allowing the shoe to be no heavier on the inner side. I use two nails on the inner side, two at the toe, and four on the outer side, and I take care to fit the toe nicely.—*By* C. H. M.

Shoeing to Prevent Interfering.

My experience is that all horses that interfere are not cured by the same shoeing. Turning the ankle in or out, as most smiths are in the habit of doing, has different effects upon different horses. The result depends entirely upon the action of the animal and the manner of striking. My method in most cases is to pare the foot to the shape given it by nature as nearly as possible. Then I fit the shoes, rights and lefts, leaving the inside of the shoe straighter than the wall of the foot.

If the season of the year is such that the ground is icy,

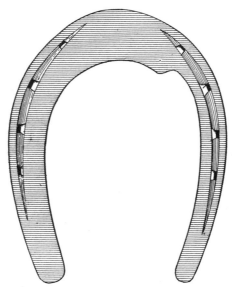

Fig. 96—A Shoe Made by " R. A. M." for Interfering Horses.

I turn the outside instead of the inside calks, as the snow path is always deepest in the middle. For this reason the outside calks strike first and so stop the tendency to slide and thus strike the other ankle. Another advantage in turning the outside instead of the inside calk is that the horse is less liable to injure himself by calking. I nail the shoe to fit the outside and toe, and fit both heels the same as in shoeing, unless the horse toes out. In that case I turn the inside calk under more. I take good care to drive the nails on the inside of the foot high and clinch smooth. The hoof is then rasped smooth and left a little flush on the shoe. This remedy, I find, very rarely fails to cure.—*By* C. H. W.

Toe-Tips—A Shoe for Interfering Horses.

My way of shoeing a horse that interferes is as follows: I take a very wide webbed shoe, as shown in the illustration, Fig. 96, and cut it the length I want it. I then split the inside bar of the shoe from about the corner of the toe to the heel, taking off about one-third the weight of the inside of the shoe, which, when properly put on, makes the horse travel wider. I never knew this shoe to fail in any case.—*By* R. A. M.

To Shoe an Overreaching Horse.

The horses that overreach are our best travelers, if properly shod and trained. If a horse overreaches badly, I put on each front foot from a $1\frac{1}{2}$ to a 2-pound shoe and a $\frac{1}{2}$-pound shoe behind, and set them out full in front at the toe. The shoes should all be made good length and wide at the heel. I never use any front shoes on any horse, but hind shoes for both hind and front feet, and I make a great many shoes.

When it comes to horses that overreach I make the shoes narrow and thick in order to get the weight in them.

This is my reason for using the heavy shoe. It is simply to make the horse carry the fore feet out of the way of the hind ones.—*By* D. J. C.

Shoeing Forging or Overreaching Horses.

In shoeing a horse to prevent forging or overreaching, I use for the front feet a toe-weight shoe made as shown in Fig. 97 of the accompanying illustration for Winter wear, and a flat shoe for Summer. I get the weight chiefly in front of the point of the frog, and draw out the quarters and heels to about the size of an ordinary medium hind

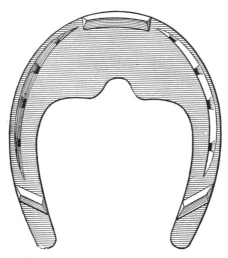

Fig 97—Temple's Method of Shoeing Forging or Overreaching Horses. A Shoe for a Front Foot.

shoe. 1 next weld on a good-sized toe calk, then take two of the next smaller size calks, heat, cut off one-half the length, weld them on slanting about an inch from the point of the heel, and round off the heels ; this removes all the sharp corners. In fitting I don't cut the heels short, but allow them to project beyond the foot well, for these shoes will tend to throw the feet far ahead, thus preventing the horse from clicking and pulling them off.

In order to open the gait behind I make a side-weight shoe as for a front foot that interferes, but make it of lighter iron and extend it well back, making the heels quite

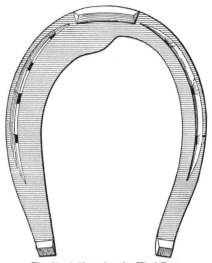

Fig. 98—A Shoe for the Hind Foot.

stiff as shown in Fig. 98. I put but three nails on the inside, starting the crease well back of the toe so that the

Fig. 99—Showing the Old Way of Welding Toes on Second hand Shoes.

third nail-hole will come opposite the fourth of the outside. This makes the shoe less liable to break near the weld of the toe calk.—*By* TEMPLE.

CHAPTER VIII.

Quarter Cracks and Split Hoofs.

A crack in the hoof is always a difficult trouble for the shoer to contend with unless he has had considerable experience in this direction. In this chapter is presented a variety of methods of treatment both for quarter cracks and split hoofs.

To Cure Quarter Cracks.

Quarter cracks are longitudinal fissures in the hoof near the heel. They are generally caused by improper shoeing or neglect of the foot, or by allowing the horse to stand on hard floors for a length of time, or by the overgrowth of the crust, or when by the paring away of the frog, sole and bars, the heel has been weakened, or by the burning of the feet in shoeing, or the springing of the shoe at the heels which then throws the weight of the horse on the wings or quarter of the coffin bone and causes the hoof to become dry and brittle.

All these things produce a disposition in the hoof to contract and when this occurs at a time when it is dry and inflexible it results in lesion or splitting.

In speedy horses where the heels are allowed to grow too high, the crust loses its elastic toughness and becomes hard and thickened and there is a liability that the repeated shock of alighting on the heel while in violent action will burst the quarters—the break occurring where the stress falls heaviest, back of the heel or at one or both sides.

In paring a foot of this kind reduce the crust, especially

at the heel, as much as it can be without injuring the foot. The contracting tendency in the hoof must be removed by rasping at the quarters until serum appears, after which the crack should be opened on both sides with a drawing knife or farrier's knife, so that friction of the fractured parts may be avoided. Then rasp or cut out the bottom of the quarter that is cracked so that no part of it may bear

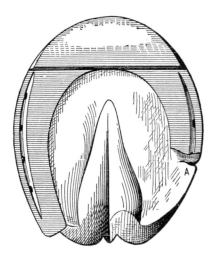

Fig. 94—Showing the Shoe to be Used when the Crack is on One Side Only.

upon the shoes. After the wall has been lowered, should the frog project below the bottom of the foot, pare it flat. By so doing the frog will be aided in growing wider and will assist the foot in expanding.

When the crack occurs well back at the heels I sometimes find it necessary to protect the weak part from concussion by applying the bar shoe. Commence thinning the shoe at the center of the quarters carrying it off both toward the heel and toward the toe, making the shoe light and the bar wide so as to obtain a strong frog pressure.

When cracks occur opposite the wings of the coffin-bone, level the foot and shorten the toe as much as it can be conveniently. If the crack occurs on one side only use the shoe shown in Fig. 94, of the accompanying illustrations.

Fig. 95—Showing the Shoe Used when the Toe and Heel Calks are Required,

If the cracks happen on both sides, shoe with a three-quarter tip, and file or rasp the wall on both sides of the crack from the coronet to the ground surface as thin as safety will permit. If toe and heel calkins are required, apply the shoe shown in Fig. 95, which is well rolled on the ground surface. If the foot be sore and tender I use meat fryings or salty lard, applying it over the hoof and sole. This will soften the wall or crest and will also strengthen the hoof. The lard should be applied every day. The new growth may also be stimulated by keeping the hoof moist with cold water bandages at night or when the animal is not in use, until the soreness is gone. Remove the shoe every three weeks in order to prevent an excessive growth of hoof.

By following these directions this form of disease may be easily and permanently cured. The time required to effect

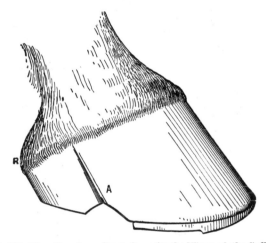

Fig. 96—Side View Showing a Crack Opposite the Wings of the Coffin Bone.

a cure is generally six months. The improvement commences at the top of the hoof and goes downward. In dressing the crack treat it as you would a crack in your hands. Cut the corners off next to the crack. The shoe shown in Fig. 94 is well beveled at the toe and cut off forward of the seat of lameness at *A*. Fig. 96 is a side view of a foot with the crack opposite the wings of the coffin-bone

A. It will be observed that the toe is well rolled or beveled, and that the heel is properly cut for the bearing at the quarters.— *By* W. C. ROBINSON.

Practical Observations on Horseshoeing.

Weak quarters and quarter cracks in horses' hoofs are a source of trouble and annoyance to a great many horse owners. Some horses can be partially cured of these ailments, while others are incurable. The owner of a horse is, of course, always desirous of using him if possible, and when a horse cannot be cured, the next thing to consider is how to ease the pain as much as possible. The following description of shoes, Fig. 97, has been proven in practice to answer a very good purpose : Select a shoe of the right

Fig. 97—Shows "C. S.'s" form of Shoe for Quarter Cracks.

size, thin down the side where the difficulty exists, and weld on a side calk forward of the weak spot or crack. Bend down the thin portion of the shoe back of the side calk. The leverage between the side calk and the toe is short, hence there will be no spring. The heel of the shoe being thin, and projecting back of the side calk, becomes a protection to that part of the foot against stones, and prevents bruising. The heel, not touching the metal, does not receive the jar when the foot comes down, and the internal mechanism of this portion of the foot is protected. I don't advise any smith to use this kind of a shoe till convinced by thorough examination of its merits. Then go ahead. It is noticeable in horseshoeing that a good hammerman is often a poor fitter. A smith with bungling movements oftentimes turns out the finest work.—*By* C. S.

Treatment of Quarter Crack.

My treatment of quarter crack is as follows : I take a thin piece of steel and draw one edge sharp ; heat it to a white heat and make a cross-cut long enough to be sure that the crack will not extend around it ; have it in a line with the shape of the crack between the hoof and the hair. The hot steel will sear it so that the foot will not bleed. Keep the hoof growing with some kind of hoof ointment. When it grows down, as it will in a few months, the quarter crack will be cured. I have cured a great many horses in this way.—*By* F. T. M.

Treating Quarter Cracks.

The first thing I do in quarter crack is to clean out the fissure as well as possible, but without cutting away any of the hoof. Next I cut about three-fourths, or an inch above the bottom of the hoof, a little notch about three-fourths of an inch from the crack on each side, and then with a brad·awl drill holes to meet across the crack, as deep as is safe, insert a good strong rivet, say $\frac{1}{8}$ inch, or a little less and draw up tight. I then put in another, above, lighter of course, as the judgment directs. I shoe the horse as usual except that the shoe must be heavy enough to prevent springing, and be well fitted to the foot, and the quarter or heel that is broken loose must be pared off so that it will bear very little if any of the shoe. I then take a $\frac{1}{2}$-inch chisel, drive it through a piece of shoe leather so the sharp edge will project about $\frac{1}{8}$ or $\frac{3}{16}$ of an inch, place the edge of the chisel just at the edge of the hair, where the new hoof begins to form, and square across the crack, and give it a tap with the hammer enough to start the blood nicely. After that I see that the shoeing is not neglected and that it is kept well riveted.

I have treated a number of cases in this way, and have never yet failed to effect a cure as soon as the hoof could grow down.

With regard to forcing the growth of the hoof with ointments, etc., I seldom recommend it in case of quarter cracks, as I think the hoof is weakened by forced or unnatural growth.—*By* F. W. S.

Shoeing Horses with Quarter Cracks.

It is a very easy matter to cure a foot with a quarter crack, and work the horse every day. My plan is as follows: I put on a bar shoe first; I then pare and fit the foot, and then rasp the quarter away so that when the shoe is on it will not touch the quarter when the horse's weight is upon it. I then take a piece of steel and draw it to a sharp edge, like a lance, and with it I burn the top of the crack in the edge of the hair. I take care that it is burned to the quick. This done I apply some tar, or good hoof ointment, to take away the soreness and to prevent taking cold in the foot. When the shoe has been on long enough to allow the quarter to grow down so that it touches the shoe, it is necessary to dress it again and reset the shoe. I take care not to let the quarter touch the shoe until it has grown down. Accordingly, some preparation to stimulate growth is desirable. For this purpose I prepare a hoof ointment which has proved to be very valuable. With it I am able to overcome the worst crack I have ever seen, in the space of four months' time, and that without the horse limping at all after the first shoeing. I commenced shoeing when I was but twelve years old, and in my time have worked in a great many different shops. I sometimes think I would rather have horses with quarter cracks, or lame, come to my shop, than those that are sound, for I know by experience that when I get one of the former, I am sure to give satisfaction to the owner.—*By* G. E. R.

Curing a Split Foot.

My way of curing a split hoof is to level the foot, making the heels as low as possible, and the sole moderately thin. I then cut a groove in the bottom of the crust of the toe, make a bar shoe, and let the bar rest on the frog so as to get a strong frog pressure. I set the toe well back on the shoe so as to get the pressure off the toe, and make the toe on the shoe long to secure a wide bearing. I use plenty of nails, but put them well back from the toe. The shoe is made rather large, and is wide at the heels. I take as much pressure off the toe as possible, keep the crack clean, and keep plenty of pine tar on the sole and wall of the foot. The shoes are kept on as long as possible. They should not be set, but should be tightened when necessary to keep them from getting loose.

An old smith came into my shop the other day, and after watching me as I cooled off a shoe to fit it, said I never would make a horseshoer in my life, because no man who did not burn the foot could get a level bearing. I asked him if he had ever dissected a horse's foot to see what it was composed of, and he said common sense would teach any man what it was—it was composed of hoof, of course. That is just about as much as some smiths know.—*By* W. A. GLAZIER.

Shoeing a Split Foot.

In shoeing a split foot, my plan is to take a shoe of the size of the foot and weld a piece from calk to calk and weld clips on the shoe in three different places—one at the toe, and one at each side of the shoe as shown in the accompany-

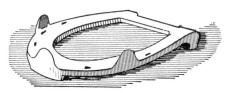

Fig. 98—" J. P. A.'s " Method of Shoeing a Split Foot.

ing illustration, Fig. 98. After driving two heel nails on each side I close carefully the clips on the side of the shoes. They should fit closely against the hoof at the bottom and should be sunk in, on a level with the outside surface of the hoof, and when they are closed neatly to the side of the hoof, you will find that the crack will close to a certain extent, but the shoe should be smaller than the foot in order to fit it after the crack is closed. Drive your other nails, then draw in your toe clevis, and file with your rasp a nick across the split. Make a deep notch at the upper end of the crack, and down to the bottom. It will split no farther, and if the shoe is kept on all the time will finally grow together.—*By* J. P. A.

Shoeing a Split Foot.

I would like to give my way of shoeing for toe cracks. Last Summer one of my customers came to my shop with a valuable horse walking on three legs—I mean that the horse walked on three legs, not the customer. I found that the right front foot was split from the coronet casing down to the bottom of the foot. The shell was in two pieces like an ox's foot, and blood was running out of it in streams. The man had been plowing, and in turning the horse had stepped with his left foot on the inside wing of the right shoe, thereby, tearing the foot apart. I went to

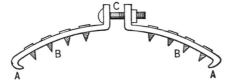

Fig. 99—A Device of "C. N. S." for Shoeing a Split Foot.

work and made two pieces of iron, as shown in the accompanying illustration, Fig. 99, and fastened one on each side of the crack, and then put a three-sixteenth inch tire-bolt through it and tightened it together. I then took a five-eighth chisel and cut a gash crosswise on the top. The foot is now in good condition. The pieces *A A*, in the illustration, are two little hooks to be burnt into the foot, *B B* are little screws, and *C* is a tire-bolt.—*By* C. N. S.

Shoeing a Cracked Hoof—Shoeing Hoof-bound Horses —Making Calks.

My way of shoeing a cracked hoof is to drive one or two brass nails through the crack, as shown in Fig. 100, and clinch on either side well to hold the crack together.

For hoof-bound horses I use a light shoe and drive it out

well at the heels. I do not pare the bars or sole more than just enough for a seat for the shoe to let the sole and frog come as low to the ground as possible when the horse steps on it. I make the shoe wide at the heels. I do not often put calks on the shoes. For a common shoe I make the calks as follows:

I take old sickle sections, cut them in the shape shown in Fig. 101, and the same size as calks, except that they are

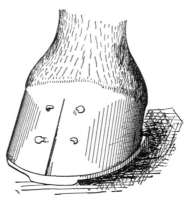

Fig. 100—Geo. Kindschi's Method of Shoeing a Cracked Hoof.

a little longer; then drive them in the shoe at the side of the calk, as shown in Fig. 102, and weld them on well. They are sure to wear sharp.—*By* GEO. KINDSCHI.

How to Shoe a Split Foot.

The horse's hoof is so constructed that any exertion may be best carried on by a certain amount of elasticity from the quarters to the point of the toe. Should, however, the natural condition of the foot be altered, by it being deprived of sufficient moisture to preserve in it the required degree of toughness and flexibility, the foot loses its power to yield to pressure and return to its shape, and when force sufficient to overcome its resistance is exerted, the hoof, no longer elastic, suddenly gives away by splitting. This occurs wherever the strain is the greatest; at either of the sides from the quarters to the heel, or directly through the

Fig. 101—Showing an Improved Calk as made by Mr. Kindschi.

middle of the hoof in front. The conditions generally present, then, in a split hoof, are a hardness, dryness and brittleness, and they may arise from various causes. For examples: Hot fitting of shoes; clipping; high toes and heels on shoes which prevent the frog from coming in contact with the ground; high heels on the foot or shoe; flat feet and long toes on draught horses; the paring away of the frog, sole, bars or heel, whereby the foot becomes contracted, are all liable to result in the splitting of the hoof.

Feet in this state are exposed to fracture either on their anterior or their lateral surfaces; with these conditions toe-crack is produced by the foot acquiring an uneven ground surface, and being thrown into an unnatural or forced posi-

Fig. 102—Showing the Method of using the Piece shown in Fig. 101.

tion. If the heel of the foot, through ignorance or neglect, is suffered to grow to an unusual height, the pressure and thrust of the coffin-bone against the comparatively thin crust, will almost always result in a fracture in front.

A peculiar accident to which horses are sometimes liable

will, also, produce the same result. When a horse shod with heel calkins overreaches himself, that is, treads on his hoof with another foot and bruises the coronet or crust, the crease thus made often extends itself until the crust is entirely split.

Toe cracks generally attack the feet of heavy draught horses. This is doubtless owing to the careless method of applying their shoes, as well as to the fact that in drawing heavy loads a greater stress is placed upon their toes than

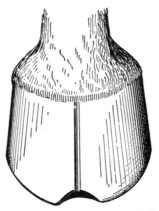

Fig. 103—Showing How the Groove is Cut at the Toe in Shoeing for Split Hoof.

upon those of other horses. In treating this disease the first care must be to thoroughly cleanse the foot, after which the crack must be pared out smoothly on either side of the crack as deep as the horny substance extends, thus widening the crevice so as to prevent all friction between the separated parts of the wall. Pressure must be taken entirely off the toe, and a groove, as shown in Fig. 103 of the accompanying illustrations, should be cut into the bottom of the crust at the toe.

Having done this, if the foot be contracted at the heel,

pare it to a level. The toe of the foot is then in turn to be
shortened and the heel weakened by paring out the commissures between the bars and frog as much as in the judgment of the farrier the foot can safely bear. The shoe represented in Fig. 104 should be used upon horses intended
for draught purposes, the nails being placed from the
front of the quarters toward the heel.

The toe calkin being placed well back from the toe, light-
ens the stress at the point where its weakness is the great-

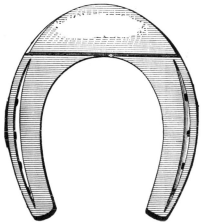

Fig. 104—A Shoe Suitable for Draught Horses.

est, and allows an easier play of the foot when in motion.
When the split occurs in the foot of a horse used for general
business work, lower the heel and shorten the toe as much
as safety will permit and thin the heel of the shoe to obtain
strong frog pressure, removing the pressure around the toe
of the foot as before directed.—*By* W. O. ROBINSON.

Curing a Split Hoof.

I give herewith a simple way of curing a split hoof.
In commencing the job, I make an awl two and one-half

inches long and as large as a No. 6 or 7 nail. I make it
oval, with a sharp point and sharp edges on the point and
do not temper it because the horse may jump and break it.
I put it in a handle four or five inches long and bore a hole

A

Fig. 105—Nail for a Split Hoof.

with it as high up on the hoof as possible. I begin a half
or a quarter of an inch from the split and bore as deep as
the horse will stand. I bore the hole to the split or crack
large enough to take the nail without much driving. I
then make a nail of the shape shown in Fig. 105 of the illustrations presented herewith. I then squirt oil in the hole,
drive the nail through the other side of the split and clinch

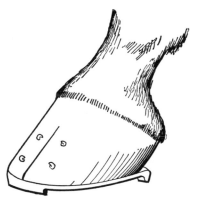

Fig. 106—Showing How the Nails are Placed.

it. I sometimes put in three nails, one above the other, and
sometimes, if the foot is sore or tender, I bore the holes on
both sides, and after the nail or nails are in I let the helper
hold up the other foot and hold a thin hot iron across the

crack at the edge of the hair until the horse feels it and gets uneasy ; then the job is done. The shoe must be kept tight, and as the foot grows down other nails must be put in, if it is necessary. I have never failed to cure when the horse was brought to my shop often enough for the foot to grow down. It makes no difference whether the crack is in the center or the front or in the quarters near the heel. The cure is certain in any case. But the nails should not be made too large. Fig. 106 shows how the nails are placed.—*By* C. H.

Shoeing Split Hoofs.

I have had a good deal of experience with cracked hoofs, and have tried a good many methods. My favorite one is a clamp shoe in which the clamps are welded to either side of a ring shoe in order to come over the front of the foot, with ease, so that a bolt can be used.

I have tried the plan of screwing on over the crack but it failed. The best and only safe plan that I have found is to drive a good light horse nail through the crack and draw it up occasionally. I have never failed by this method. Sometimes I have put as many as three nails in one hoof. Quarter cracks are much harder to cure than a front one, for they so often lap. I use a ring shoe for a quarter crack and cut away the quarter so it does not rest on the shoe. This keeps the crack from spreading while the horse is traveling. Sometimes for bad cracks I calk at the edge of the hair. — *By* C. E. C.

Curing a Split Hoof.

My plan for curing a split hoof can be explained in a few words. It is to weld on each side of the shoe, near the heel, a piece of iron of sufficient length to come up over

the foot a little more than half way to the hair. Then I
make a hole in the ends to put a small bolt through. I al-

Fig. 107—" E.'s " Device for Curing a Split Hoof.

ways use a good solid shoe. The straps should be light
enough to bend readily. The length can be taken with a
piece of paper. The accompanying illustration, Fig. 107,

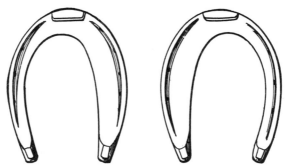

Fig. 108—C. W. Kohler's Shoe for Interfering Horses.

will give a clear idea of my plan. Rivets can be used to
draw the crack together, but in using rivets care must be
taken to avoid going too deep.—*By* R.

Shoeing for Interfering, and for Split Feet.

Fig. 108, of the accompanying illustrations, represents a pair of shoes intended to prevent a horse from knocking its knees or interfering in front.

First level the feet, then make the shoes twice as heavy on the inside as on the outside but of even thickness. Then fit the shoes to the feet and don't cut anything off the inside wall.

Fig. 109 represents my method of shoeing a split foot.

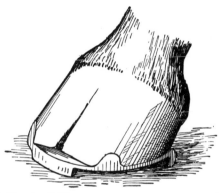

Fig. 109—Showing C. W. Kohler's Method of Shoeing a Split Foot.

Clip the shoe on each side near the front, trim the sole very thin at the crack and cut out the wall as shown in the illustration so that the shoe won't bear on the crack.—*By* CHAS. W. KOHLER.

Shoeing a Split Foot.

My way of shoeing a split foot is to first remove all the dirt from it, then drive a nail through the hoof about one and a half inches on each side of the split, then bend the head up, and put a piece of wire (I use hay bale wire) twice around the nail. If the wire proves to be a little too long take it off, twist it until it is short enough, then put it on and hammer the nail head back toward the point of the nail.

Fig. 110—Method of Shoeing a Split Hoof.

Having in this way drawn the split firmly together, as in the illustration, Fig. 110, I fire the hoof and it will then grow out. This method has never failed. After firing use some healing ointment.—*By* "SUBSCRIBER."

Shoeing a Split Hoof.

My way of shoeing a split foot is to make a shoe with clips from the hind quarter rim to the front and close enough for a three-inch bolt to join them. I then make in each clip a hole large enough for a half-inch bolt, and then pare the hoof and with the edge of a rasp file a notch about two inches long across the hoof and just where the bolt crosses. This notch is cut into with a knife until it bleeds and the bolt is then put in and drawn as tightly as the horse can bear, see Fig. 111. Twice a week tighten, drawing the bolt a little tighter than it was before.   Keep this shoe on until the crack grows half the way down and then put on an ordinary shoe.

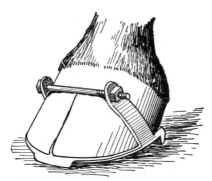

Fig. 111—Device for Shoeing a Split Hoof.

This plan has cured every case I have ever treated.—*By* H. T. GALL.

CHAPTER IX.

SHOEING KNEE-SPRUNG, FLAT-FOOTED OR CLUB-FOOTED HORSES, ETC.

Shoeing a Knee-sprung or Flat-footed Horse.

In the case of a horse knee-sprung from a recent strain on the back cords, I find it well to leave the heel of the foot high, and put on quite a long shoe, as that helps to relieve the cords.

I will also give my method of shoeing flat-footed horses. A flat foot, as every farrier knows, does not need much paring on the bottom; some, in fact, will bear hardly enough to even them up, the growth being straight out on the toe, and with some the bottom of the foot is very thin. If such a horse is shod with a shoe the full size of the foot, it brings the bearing too far from the center of the foot, and as the horse's weight bears mostly near the center of the foot when it is in shape, there is need to get the bearing of the foot on the shoe back as near to the center as possible. In preparing a flat foot for the shoe, I take a sharp rasp and cut the toe back as far as I think will do, and then fit my shoe the full size of what foot I leave, giving the shoe as even a bearing as possible. In shoeing this way I have helped some quite bad cases of drop sole. Any one can easily see that a heavy horse, with a thin bottom to his foot, will press the sole down quicker if the bearing on the shoe is too far away from the bones in the foot on which his weight comes.—*By* C. WEST.

Shoeing Flat-footed Horses.

To shoe a flat-footed horse, pare the bottom of the foot as little as possible at the heel, just enough to level the foot. At the toe pare off all surplus horn or hoof; avoid cutting the sole. In fitting use an ordinary front shoe. Concave it well with an oval-faced hammer. Toe it with a heavy piece of steel according to the size of shoe. Turn a good solid heel and leave the steel about one-quarter or three-eighths of an inch higher than the toe. Be particular in fitting the shoe to the foot. It is very difficult to give a definite rule for this operation, as feet differ. My explanation that follows applies to very flat feet. Fit the shoe back of the foot and round off what projects with the rasp. Some feet are made better by taking off one-half inch, giving a good chance to get a fair nail hold, bringing the heel well around to the frog in order to cover the point of horn at the heel, with the shoe. This is done to keep the heel from settling down between the ends of the shoe. This trouble is always met with in any width shoe, because it causes too much weight on the quarters of the foot.

Make the shoe perfectly level from heel to toe. The foot should be level, so that when you lay on the shoe to nail there will be no rock to it. Get as deep a nail hold as possible, so as not to break the foot.—*By* G.

Flat-footed Horses—How Should They be Shod?

Sometimes the bottom of the foot has been cut away until it becomes rounded like the top of a tortoise shell. Such a horse has large, flat feet, thin shell, or meaty foot, wide heels, thin sole, and large frog, of course. He should be shod with a wide web, thick shoe, concaved, to make the bearing come on the outer edge of the foot to protect the sole. (The owner must see to it that dirt and gravel do not get lodged under the concavity.) Now set up calks to keep the frog and sole from stones and bruising, and we have about the method that should be pursued in shoeing flat feet. Now, is anything the matter? Yes; the frog gets no bearing. Well, what of that? Why, the frog is the

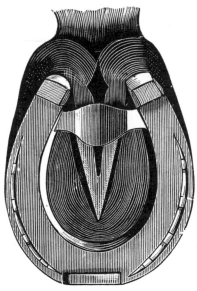

Fig. 112—Method of Applying a Spring to a Shoe for the Protection of the Frog.

cushion on which the bottom bone rests, and because the frog gets no ground bearing, the frog and sole are forced down by the weight of the horse and the rim of the foot is forced up. This is what causes the tortoise-shell shape alluded to above. The frog must have a bearing in order to prevent the foot bones from pushing through the bottom of the foot. This calls for the spring-bar, which is better than the ordinary bar shoe on account of its elasticity. Adjust the spring so that it will rest on the frog a little before the shoe touches the heels. This will give a bearing on the frog and keep the frog and sole up to their places. With this arrangement you divide the bearing between the frog and the quarters as nearly in the natural way as possible. If a horse could always rest a part of his weight on the frog, he never would suffer with contracted quarters, flat or bulged soles or tender frog (with sufficient water bathing in dry weather and while standing in dry places). But, to continue : Take a piece of steel one-thirty-second of an inch thick, cut out the frog spring long enough to put into the shoe a little forward of the heel, with sharp chisel punch. Punch a hole in the inner part of each side of the shoe three-eighths of an inch or more deep. These holes are for the ends of the spring and should be large enough to permit the spring to play a little, both endways and sideways. Cut the spring the right length after the shoe is fitted to the foot, then open the shoe and put the spring in. When the frog bears on the spring it holds the frog and sole and foot bones in their places, and the sole, if left alone, will soon thicken and harden and admit of an inner bearing. The spring should neither be tempered nor hardened. The accompanying engraving, Fig. 112, shows the spring and the manner of applying.—*By* S. STONE.

Flat Feet.

The bearing of flat feet, as a general rule, keeps the sole always on a level with the wall of the foot. Now since the walls of flat feet spread instead of growing straight down, it follows that such feet are always low enough, and no paring can be done in that direction without endangering the animal.

To shoe them I would first, with a good pair of pinchers,

cut away the overgrowth of the hoof if there is any, then simply level the bottom to receive the shoe. In paring and trimming such feet, care should be taken to always leave plenty of horn for the shoe to rest on. It is by trimming the edges of the foot too far in. in the foolish attempt to make it smaller, that all the mischief is done. You thereby deprive the foot of all wall support, and throw the whole

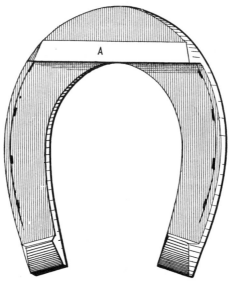

Fig. 113.—Shoe Made by " J. E. M." for Straightening a Crooked Foot.

weight of the horse on the soles of his feet, which are now higher than the wall, and you must pare them down to bring them even with the outer crust, making them thereby very thin and sensitive. If the horse works with such feet it will generate fever and diseases, among which is drop-sole. In this case, I would recommend to put the horse in a pasture for about three weeks, and see that his feet are kept moist and cool. To shoe him, if he is not too far gone, I would level up the seat of the shoe even with the sole with layers of harness leather, and then nail the shoe, which I would have tolerably wide, on top of it.—*By* A. D.

Shoeing and Straightening a Crooked Foot.

My way of shoeing and straightening a crooked foot is shown in the accompanying illustration, Fig. 113, in which I take a mule's shoe for an example, because mules are more subject to crooked feet than are horses. With this shoe I straightened, in six months, the hoof of a mule that walked on the side of his foot. If the ankle of the foot runs in, put the extension of the toe *A* on the inside of the shoe. If the ankle runs out put *A* on the outside. Fit well and tack on. It may be somewhat troublesome at first, but the animal will soon get used to it, and there is no danger of interfering.—*By* J. E. M.

Shoeing Flat-footed Horses.

Some men think that a flat-footed horse should always be shod with a bar shoe. When the foot is healthy I put on a plain shoe, well beveled on the side next to the sole as far back as the last nail-hole. Particular pains must be taken not to let the shoe bear on the sole, for, if so, it will be apt to lame the horse.

I have had many cases of lameness caused in this manner, and cured them by paring the sole a little where the shoe rested.

If the shell is chipped off on the edges so that it is not level with the sole, I place a strip of leather under the shoe all the way around the hoof. This prevents the shoe from bending itself in the shell, and allows the hoof to grow down, so that, at the next shoeing, there will be a firmer vein of horn on which to nail the shoe.—*By* HIGHLAND.

Shoeing a Crooked Foot.

I will describe my way of shoeing crooked feet. I do not cut away the toe at all. If the horse travels with his feet out, I begin at the toe and gradually thicken to the heel on the inside of the foot, or I put on a side heel calk, say three to four inches in length, with a gradual slope. By so doing I throw the inside of the foot much higher than the outside, I let the toe calk have the same slope, I raise the inside according to the crookedness of the foot and as I have no scale for their height, use my own judgment. If the horse travels with his feet in, I reverse the form of the shoe. I have never failed with this method. I never cut a foot to straighten it, for it is not the foot which needs treatment, it is the gait of the animal.

My way of shoeing is to shoe as long and as wide at the heel as the gait of the animal will permit. I never pare the sole any more than nature sheds. The frog I treat in the same way.—*By* J. B. H.

A Knee-Sprung Horse—Thrush.

My plan for winter shoeing of knee-sprung horses is to pare the foot at the toe, as in ordinary shoeing. Keep the heel down rather low, and let the shoe stick out over the heel a little more than usual.

For spring or summer, I shoe perfectly flat, and find that then the horse always goes well.

I had a case of thrush last summer, and cured it by the following treatment: I poured kerosene oil into the frog of the foot twice a day, and applied fine salt for two days, taking care to keep the feet out of the wet when the horse was standing. The cure was speedy and thorough.—*By* UN-KNOWN.

Club Feet.

Crooked foot or club foot is a disease often neglected by both the horse owner and the shoer. Colts are sometimes foaled with crooked feet, allowed to grow to three or four

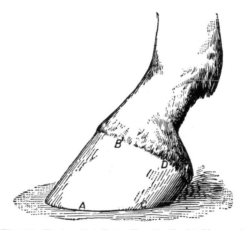

Fig. 114—Shoeing Club Feet. How the Hoof is Measured.

years of age without any attention, and are consequently almost ruined for the market and even for general work. Crooked feet should be attended to as soon as the colt is of sufficient strength to admit of handling. We should look after our colts' feet from the time they are by the side of the mother, until they arrive at the age when it becomes necessary to have shoes put on their hoofs.

Horseshoers, as a general rule, neglect paring the feet level and straight as they should be in every case, for when

the feet are crooked they are out of balance, and this also
brings a constant strain on the joints. Keep your horse's
feet straight, of an even length on the sides and at the
quarters, and then apply a shoe with an even bearing on
the wall.

Always keep a pair of compasses in your shoeing box,
and measure the hoof as shown in the accompanying illus·
tration, Fig. 114, from *A* to *B* on either side of the toe, and

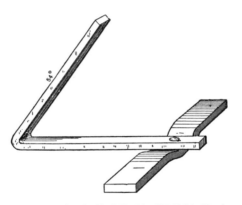

Fig. 115—Showing the Tool Used by "J. C." in Shoeing.

from *C* to *D* at the quarters, then make a tool like the one
shown in Fig. 115, to indicate the degrees at which a foot
should stand, and you will have no trouble in balancing the
foot properly. The hoof should be set at about 54 to 56
degrees. This tool is made of three pieces of iron riveted
together as follows : Front, 4 inches; bottom, 5 inches; cross-
piece, 6 inches long. The bottom piece is curved as shown
in Fig. 115. The diagram, Fig. 116, is given to show the
correct angle so that a blacksmith who wishes can make a
tool accurately from this angle.—*By* J. C.

Shoeing with Tips—Shoeing Stumbling and Knee-Sprung Horses—Shoeing for Corns.

As regards shoeing with tips, I think it depends upon the nature of the foot to be shod. If the heel is low, there is generally a good healthy frog, and in most cases a light sole, and consequently the tips could not be let into the foot. In my practice I find that tips are a good thing for

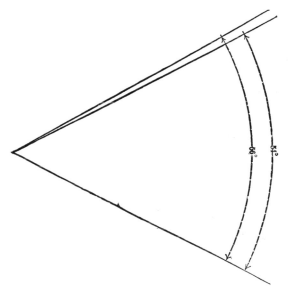

Fig. 116—Diagram used by "J. C." to Show the Correct Angle.

some feet. For instance, if a foot is contracted at the heels and has a high wall and the foot is hard, and there is a thick hard sole and a small hard frog, pinched on either side by the bars, then I say put on tips. I make the tips of steel, and taper them down from the toe to the heel, having the heel half as thick as the toe, but making the heel inserted somewhat at about the center of the quarter. This gives the foot a level bearing. I know that tips put on horses with feet as I have described, had the desired effect, that is, they widened the heels. And the horses did not become lame although they were driven over paved streets all the Summer months.

My method of shoeing a stumbling horse is as follows: Shoe with plates, rasp off the toe of the foot, then put the hot shoe in the vise at the first toe nails, and turn it up to fit the toe of the foot.

I think all competent horseshoers will maintain that a knee-sprung horse should be raised on his or her heels. If there is plenty of hoof, I pare off the toe and then put on a common shoe. If there is not plenty of hoof, and the heels are low, the desired height should be made up in the heel of the shoe. If a toe calk is needed it should be hammered down low.

In shoeing a horse with corns the best way is to cut off the heel of the shoe on the inside, as the heel is the most subject to corns. Do not pare down the heel or bar, but leave them in contact with the ground and your horse will then have a good sound heel.—*By* J. J. McN.

Stumbling Horses.

To shoe horses that stumble, pare the foot as for ordinary shoeing and nail the shoe on pointing forward, as you think the foot should be carried in traveling. Horses that stumble generally have a round or wide foot and toe in. This causes them to hit the foot that stumbles on the hoof, just back of the fourth nail from the toe, with the side of the other foot. The blow is so light that it leaves scarcely any mark, but it will soon produce soreness at the point struck and cause the horse to stumble very often. Point the shoe straight forward, therefore, and remove the side of the hoof all it will bear.—*By* D. N.

Curing a Turned Foot.

I will give you my remedy for treating a hind foot that is turned. I have never treated front feet. I take a new shoe, fit it in the ordinary way, and then take a piece of old wagon spring about $1\frac{1}{2}$ inches wide, and weld to the bottom of the toe of the shoe, taking care to cut it so long that it will come to the top of the hoof and bend almost like a sleigh runner, leaving the calkin about 2 inches long. I then turn the animal out, as it would under no circumstances do to use him. Bathing frequently with some of the many liniments will be beneficial. The shoe should be taken off every three or four weeks, or as often as necessary, and the runner made sharper in the bend and the calkins cut down gradually until the foot comes to the proper shape.—*By* S. E. G.

To Prevent Striking.

To prevent a horse from striking his front feet with the hind ones, I put on the front feet, shoes that are very heavy, but a little shorter than the common style. On the hind feet I use very light shoes, and, if they are calked, set the calk pretty far back in the shoe. I then set the shoes so that the hoof will project a little in front of them. After shoeing a horse in this way a few times, he may afterward be shod like any other horse, and will travel right.—*By* C. L. D.

Curing a Clicking Horse.

My method of curing a clicker, that is, a horse that strikes his hind feet against the front ones is as follows :

I take a pair of front shoes a size too large (I use Juniata shoes when I can get them) and make spring heels on them. I fit them as long as usual and put on heavy toe calks but forge the toes down until they are no higher than the heels,

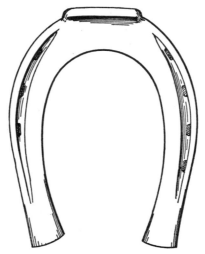

Fig. 117—The Shoe Used for Curing a Clicking Horse.

as shown in the accompanying illustration, Fig. 117. I fit the shoe level. For the hind feet I use the smallest shoe I can make to answer and fit as in front except that I leave the toe as high again as in front. This never fails to stop a horse from clicking. It is a habit, in my opinion, and the horse acquires it because he chooses to do so, not because he cannot help it.—*By* I. N. BAILEY.

What is a Founder?

The trouble popularly known as " founder " is described in works on veterinary surgery as *laminitis,* or an inflammation of the foot. This disease appears in two forms. In the simple form the sensitive lamina of the foot and the equally sensitive sole are affected, while in the more severe form the bones of the foot are also included. Among the many causes of this disease, perhaps the most common is the severe concussion from fast driving on hard roads, over-

Fig. 118—Form of Shoe for Foundered Horses.

exertion and over-feeding, and drinking cold water when the horse is heated. The treatment recommended by eminent authorities, consists in the administration of mild purgatives : tincture of aconite in small and repeated doses, as a febrifuge, with poultices to the foot in the early stages of the disease and cold applications later. Use a form of shoe such as is shown in Fig. 118. "As early as possible, get lightly nailed on the feet affected, extremely stout, wide-webbed and long-bar shoes, made from iron about twice the ordinary thickness that the particular horse's shoes are made from ; make them gradually thin from behind the quarters, so that the heel part of the shoes is wide and thin, and fitted rocker fashion, which enables the horse to throw his weight where he tries to, much better than he can in ordinary shoes or without any ; that is, off the pedal bone on to the soft elastic tissues and tendon behind it, which are much less vascular and sensitive."—*American Agriculturist.*

Shoeing Chest-Foundered Horses.

Let such a chest foundered horse go barefoot, in order to wear off his toes. If the heels fail to wear off so as to get the frog bearings sufficient to spread the heel, cut them down until the frog will get its portion of the bearing. When the toe wears so as to become tender on the bottom put on a thin shoe for a time and let the growth continue. Then take off the light shoes and let the horse go barefoot again.

The heels and frogs on such horses will never suffer without a shoe. Just a tip, or half shoe, will be sufficient in most cases. From this it will be noticed that my idea of shoeing chest-foundered horses does not consist in not shoeing them at all, but in not shoeing as much as is the usual custom. Let the horse's feet have plenty of water, and let the foot gradually come into natural shape and proportion, with reference to amount of heel and toe, so that the joints can come to a natural position. The horse's feet will then gradually come back under him and the so-called chest-founder will gradually disappear.

The points to be borne in mind are the water, the natural shape of foot, the frog bearing, position of joints and position of leg. The pastern and coffin joints are usually the sufferers, aside from the contraction of shell upon the wings of paddle bones, where corns usually commence. The inflammation here contracts the hoof still more and makes the back cord sore. These causes lead to a long high toe in proportion to the heel. This is generally termed chest-founder. The horse sets his feet forward, and the breast appears to fall in because the shoulders are forward.—*By* S. S.

Drop Sole or Pumice Foot.

Drop sole arises from various causes. It may come from founder or laminitis, or it may come with some horses from heavy work and improper shoeing. The case I have in view now arose from the last-named cause. The horse on a heavy pull would do his work with the toe of the shoe. He had been examined and shod by a great many smiths, some of whom would call the trouble by one name, some by another. The owner labored under the impression that the horse was hoof-bound. I made an examination and found the hoof tender and broken loose at and around the point of the frog, the toe being long and showing a tendency to turn up. The horse pulled with his toe or the toe of the shoe, and the toe of the hoof being long, the strain caused the back part of the laminæ to elongate, and the weight pressed against the sole causing it to flatten and draw the horny sole from the sensitive or fleshy sole. The crust or outside wall had lost its proper form and become flatter, appearing as if it were forced upward from the ground.

So much as regards the cause of the disease and the appearance of the hoof. Now as to the shoeing. It is first necessary to shorten the toe as much as possible without injury, as the sole in this condition is weak. Care must be taken not to cut or pare in any way more than is necessary for the proper levels of the shoe. When the foot is thus prepared a shoe, such as is shown in Fig. 113, page 202, is to be applied. By having the toe *A* set well back on the shoe, the center of gravity will fall more directly on the foot and leg bones, and the strain will be taken off the injured parts. Reset the shoes every four weeks, and in a few shoeings the sole will return to its natural concaved form. Any application to promote the growth of the hoof is good. Before the application of this shoe the horse, after being driven three miles on a hard road and put in the stable over night, could hardly get out of the stable again. After this shoe had been applied the horse was driven thirty miles on a hard road, put in stable over night, and the next morning came out as free from soreness as when he was put in.

Drop sole has other causes besides those I have mentioned. Springing the shoe off at the heels and breaking down the quarters will also cause drop sole on heavy draught horses that have low, broad heels.—*By* J. E. M.

Shoeing to Correct Forging.

The difference in weight and gait of horses requires some slight difference in the method of shoeing with regard to the weight and length of shoe to be used. Some horses can carry a two-pound shoe quite conveniently, while an equal weight would tell very materially upon other horses after a few miles of travel. It is noticed that speeding horses oftentimes have the fault of forging more or less. The continual disagreeable sound that is heard when speeding is anything but satisfactory to drivers' ears, and the resistance to the forward movement of the foot by the blow must, of course, suddenly check the forward movement of the limb. The heels of a horse that are battered and scarified after a severe drive cannot but engage the attention of the owner, if present. Some assert that it is impossible to stop a horse from forging when badly addicted to the habit. This opinion, however, is not altogether accepted by horsemen, and every possible means that can be employed in the limit ed sphere of shoeing is brought to bear on the case, so that, if possible, the fault may be remedied.

The close attention of the driver to the planting of the foot shows that if the front foot could be caused to slightly lengthen the stride the forging would cease. Therefore take the practical observation of the driver and make use of it. It is well understood in mechanics that accelerated momentum will carry a weight quite a distance. For instance, a person not weighted, who can jump eight feet, can jump nearly a foot farther with dumb-bells. This principle is applicable to a certain extent to the front limbs of the forging horse. Let the toe of the shoe be heavy. Let the smith use his own good judgment as to the weight. One shoeing may not suffice. Note the effect of the first experiment and be governed by it in subsequent operations.

Some smiths advocate a long shoe. By this means the weight would be at the heels. If the extra weight is at the toe on the shoe a neater job is made. Have the heels short and beveled under, with a broad chamfer along the quarter. Make the chamfer while the shoe is hot. A slight filing makes it bright when cold. For fine work one inch back of crust termination is amply sufficient for hoof bearings. The shoe should be concaved on the bottom or heavily chamfered. No nail heads should project out of the crease. A front clip has its advantages and disadvantages. It depends very much upon the judgment of the shoer whether it should be used or not.

The hind shoes require to be as high as the circumstances admit. The toe calk should be hot-filed of all projecting and superfluous metal. If the evil is stopped by having a full toe, so much the better; if not, regulate the toe by hot-filing, and set the shoe back as little as the circumstances permit. Bear in mind as you set back the shoe that you advance to a point of serious danger to the foot. Round all the sharp corners of the heels of the front shoe. When the clicking of the shoes is removed one annoyance is overcome; but more frequently a more serious one remains. To remove it has been the object of horseshoers for many years. The method here described is not guaranteed to be effective in all cases, but there are points in it which are good.—*By* C. S.

CHAPTER X.

MISCELLANEOUS SUBJECTS

Thick-Heeled Shoes.

I wish to contribute my quota of experience about a matter that is of considerable importance to our craft. The custom of applying hind shoes made very thick, or feather-edged, on the inside, was one that became prevalent from the beginning of the present century. Its supposed influence as a remedy against cutting was founded on the hypothesis that by raising the inside of the foot the pastern joint was tilted outward, which was supposed to enable the elevated foot to pass the limb planted on the ground without touching it. The same injurious practice has been more or less extended to the fore feet, on the faith of some such speculative notions. It has also been supposed that thick-heeled shoes give support to the joint and tendons ; while, again, horses are shod with the outside heel of the hind shoe turned up and the inside made thick, with the idea of giving the foot a level bearing. These belong to some of the Old World notions, which have led to the twisting of the horse's legs, the jar and injury of their feet and joints, resulting in splints, spavins, and other affections of the hock joint, all of which diseases have become prevalent through ignorant malpractice.

The objections here urged do not apply to the use of calkins, which are often useful, especially for draught horses. The safety of a sound horse in action, and when his movements are free, greatly depends on the state of his hind feet. An animal crippled on his fore feet falls and breaks his knees; but if a sound horse, free on his limbs—say an unshod colt, galloping in the field—falls, it is always through his hind feet giving way, by their slipping under him, in which case he comes down on his quarters or on his side, but not on his knees.

A little artificial aid answers the purpose of giving security to the horse in almost all emergencies.   The thick-heeled shoes both jar the horse and act like skates on his feet, and when one limb of the shoe is made thick and the other turned up, on the supposition that the horse stands level, the opposite effect follows; for although the foot may appear level whilst the animal stands on flag-stones or boards, yet the case is reversed as soon as he is put to work, whether on common roads, paved streets, or ground more or less yielding; the heel that is turned up will find or make depressions, whilst the solid, thick, inside half of the shoe remains above ground and jars the horse's limbs, becoming a source of inconvenience without one redeeming advantage. —*By* F. I. G.

To Shoe a Horse Injured by Calking.

It is very surprising to me that the mechanics in cities are, as a rule, inferior to those in the country. I do not say this because I have anything against the city mechanics, for I think they are more brotherly than the country workmen, who are always running one another down.

But let that be as it may, what I wish to speak of now is the art of horseshoeing in particular.   It seems strange that shoers have so many different ideas about shoeing the same kinds of feet.   I have seen some especially bad work in some of the Western cities,   For example: I saw a horse

that had been calked brought in one of these Western shops
to be shod and have his foot treated.   I will now explain the
nature of the calk, so that my brother smiths will understand the condition of the foot.   The calk or cut was in the
center of the fore-foot, about an inch below the hair, and
extending downward, being short but deep.   This smith, if
so he can be called, went to work as follows: He cut the
clinches and removed the shoe in the ordinary way; then
taking his paring-knife, he cut from the hair clear to the
point of the toe, or the entire length of the foot.   Understand, he cut each side of the calk, thereby making a large
cavity the shape of the letter V, leaving the flesh, or membrane, or quick, exposed to the dirt, grit and filth of the
streets, and the blood oozing out.   He then nailed on the
shoe, and pronounced the operation complete.   That horse
was then a hundred per cent worse than when he entered
the shop.

You ask, Well, how did the horse get along in this condition?   The result was simply this: dirt and gravel got in
the exposed parts, and the animal became lame, not only
on account of the dirt and gravel, but because when the
foot was put on the ground and the weight of the animal
bore down on it the cut expanded, causing great pain.

Now, any smith ought to know that the heel is the expanding or contracting portion of the foot, and, therefore,
when the front of the hoof is split to the entire length, it
will expand, causing pain and lameness.   This horse became worse at once, and the owner took him to another
shop.   I happened to be present at the time, and the smith
asked me what I thought about the treatment the foot had
received.   I told him the smith that did that job was a fool,
in my opinion, and did not understand his business; and,
furthermore, that he ought to be arrested for cruelty to
animals.   I then gave the smith a little advice as to the

way I would treat that foot; I would first cleanse the sore portions thoroughly, then make the foot perfectly water and air-tight with resin. I think resin far better than tar for this purpose, as nothing will adhere to it. After sealing the foot securely, I would apply a steel shoe that would not take and give, the foot then being perfectly solid and in no danger of expanding. Sometimes a bar-shoe is far better than an ordinary one.—*By* W. G. T.

Self-Sharpening Calks.

I will give you a description of our style of shoeing. Our country is very rough and stony, rendering an iron calk useless for fall and winter. Our summer shoeing is of but little importance, being most all resetting old shoes nearly worn out, which are expected to stay on from three

Fig. 120—Shows How Calk is Split.

to five months, at the end of which time they have the shoes tightened up and perhaps come back to have a new nail put in some vacant nail hole. To simmer the thing down fine, the smith who puts shoes on to *stay the longest* is the best shoer.

Our winter shoeing is of a different nature in quality of shoe. Then we use our self-sharpening shoe, which we put on as soon as the ground freezes, and they are kept on till spring.

To make a self-sharpening shoe, pick a shoe to fit the foot you are going to shoe, and turn down the heel calks as for mud calks. Then with a sharp flat chisel, made from a large flat file, split the calk as shown in Fig. 120. Now take the best cast steel that will harden the hardest without breaking, and make slips as shown in No. 2 of Fig. 120. They should be a trifle wider than the width of the calk, and an eighth of an inch deeper than the depth of the slit. Weld with borax, or some good compound, so as to keep

Fig. 121—Section of Shoe Showing Toe Calk.

good life in the steel. Make your toe calks of iron, then weld to shoe good and solid. Then make slips, as shown in Fig. 121, a trifle longer than the toe. Now weld, as shown, being careful to keep the steel out to the edge where the shoe is sharp. This can easily be done by filing the iron off as the toe is being drawn out, when the shoe is fitted to the foot. It is now ready for tempering, and this is my way of tempering. Heat toe and heel to a good cherry red and then cool the shoe off by dipping in water and holding it there till cool. Hold the edge of the calk in the fire and draw the temper to a copper color. Heavy mower sections, such as the Buckeye, make good slips for ice or snow roads, but are too light to stand frozen ground or stone. The steel of a circular saw is the best I have ever used.—*By* J. A. B.

Sharpening Calks—Setting Heels and Toes.

My belief is that many blacksmiths set the toe calk under instead of setting it out as it should be. After the toe is welded turn the heels in the air and sharpen from the inside of the toe with the pane of the hammer. This gives the outward slant in sharpening so the shoe is not thrown out of shape.

A horse in pulling, sets the heel down first, which makes

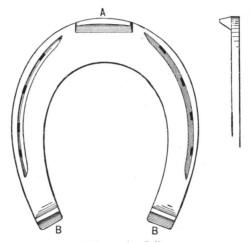

Fig. 122—Sharpening Calks.

the shoe slant, and if it slants inward the horse will slip in pulling up-hill, while if it slants outward he gets a firm hold.

Never set the heels square across. They should always be set with the curve of the shoe and then they prevent the horse from slipping sidewise. Slope them toward each other as shown in the illustration, Fig. 122, in which *B B* represents the heels and *A* the toe.—*By* H. R.

To Shoe a Horse that Crosses one Leg Over the Other.

To prevent a horse calking himself that has the fault of crossing one hind leg with the other, I employ the plan given below. I would say that three customers of mine each own a horse that had the same fault. I tried different ways to stop it, but found no way so good as to shoe them with a shoe on the foot that they crossed the other one with,

Fig. 123—Shoe to Prevent Calkiug.

similar to Fig. 123. *C* is the inside of shoe. Instead of having a calk at *A*, as on the other side, I have a calk at *B*, at the last heel nail hole. The shoe at *A* should be filed smooth; the calk at *B* should be the same kind of calk as is commonly put on heels ; have tried the above way of shoeing the horses referred to for three years, and they have not calked themselves once. — *By* RAB OF THE WYNDE.

Predmore's Rotary Clincher.

This clincher is my own invention, and comes nearer perfection than any I have seen.

The clincher complete is shown in Fig. 124. It consists of the lower handle, Fig. 125, with end mortised as shown.

In this the rotary, Fig. 126, is attached and connected with the upper handle, which is also the lower jaw, Fig. 128, by the connecting bar, Fig. 127.

In Figs. 126 and 128, the holes *D* and *C* are threaded for

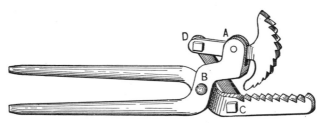

Fig. 124—Predmore's Rotary Clincher Complete.

screws, as in these holes the bolts are required to be set very firmly. The bolts may be seen at *D* and *C* in Fig. 124.

Fig. 125—Showing Lower Handle, and how the End is Mortised.

To operate, simply hold the rotary firmly to the foot, close the handles and the rotary will clinch the same as a hammer.—*By* G. W. PREDMORE.

Shall Nails be Clinched in Horseshoeing?

Does it do any good to clinch the nails in a horse's foot?

I have shod horses most of the time for thirty-five years, and have come to the conclusion that a clinch is of no use, though I still practice it, for the majority of men would feel sure the shoes would drop off unless the nails were clinched. Some of my customers, however, won't have them clinched at all.

Experience has shown me that more nails break off be-

Fig. 126—The Rotary for Clincher.

Fig. 127—The Connecting Bar for Clincher.

tween the shoe and the hoof than get loose enough to draw out.

As proof of this you will generally see the nails sticking up above the hoof when the shoe gets settled into its place, showing clearly that the shoe is not held by the clinch.

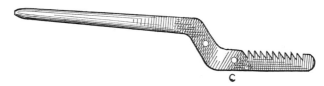

Fig. 128—The Lower Jaw for Clincher.

Nails seldom get loose enough to pull down against the clinch.

I conclude, therefore, that the time employed in clinching nails is wasted, as a shoe will stay on as long without as with clinching.—*By* S. B. PEPPER.

Driving Horseshoe Nails.

Horseshoes can be kept on a long time by the following plan. I think shoes well fitted to the foot will stay as long as they ought to remain without re-setting. But for large horses I find it works well to drive the nails as shown in the accompanying illustration, Fig. 129.—*By* L. W. P.

A Novel Idea in Horseshoeing.

I have been looking into the matter of horseshoes lately, trying for something practicable to prevent contraction,

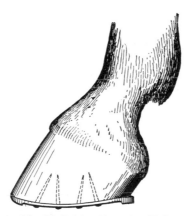

Fig. 129—Driving Horseshoe Nails.

but haven't found anything better than the generally accepted plans, unless it is Hague's Expansion Shoe.

Did you ever observe that anything that is bright, shows up very conspicuously on the feet. There was good sense in the old-fashioned shoe buckle. I think I have seen it stated that while Washington was president he rode through the streets of Philadelphia behind six splendid white horses which were shod with gold. I don't know if the Lord Mayor of London puts on that much style, but it is a matter which history has considered of sufficient importance to mention that Nero had his mules shod with silver, while those of his wife were shod with gold. A horse's hoof can be polished until it is as smooth and as glossy as a tortoise-shell comb, and it is certainly perfect taste to have them so. But that polished hoof will be set off to great advantage, and attention will be called to it if there is but the faintest bright glimmer of gold on a thin line around its base. There is no

Fig. 130—Showing Some Tasteful Designs for Artistic Horseshoeing.

necessity of this brightness being of gold, brass will answer as well. A steel shoe can be made with a channel for the insertion of brass, and arranged to show the bright brass bottom when the horse is in motion and the band of yellow metal at the base of the hoof when the horse is standing still.

The engraving, Fig. 130, conveys some idea of the fanciful effects which may be produced. Fashion makes business. Fashion is the most beneficent of all the goddesses, and if she refuses her favors to the blacksmith then he should take them. Business will be good when the product of the blacksmith is subject to the caprice of fashion.

Even putting a brass plate across the hoof, the full size and 1-16 inch thick under the shoe, turning up a flange or not, would be a benefit to horses as much as india rubber and be yielding enough to take off the jar of the hard pavement, but not enough to let the shoe move up and down sufficiently to loosen it.—*By* B. F. SPALDING.

Bar Shoes and their Uses.

It is impossible for a man to know all the good ideas of the trade. If we err in our conclusions it is no fault of the heart, but rather something that happens to the best of us sometimes. When a bar shoe is to be made the blacksmith puts his thinking cap on. He is on the threshold of vet-

Fig. 131—A Form of Bar Shoe.

erinary surgery. Of all the methods which present themselves, that which is most acceptable for the case in hand is the one sought. Practical experience opens the way for the judgment to choose. Then comes the practical test. When the crossbar of a shoe rests on the soft part or extremity of the frog it is apt to cause injury to it, but when it is placed farther towards the point it rests on the harder part of the frog, producing better results. It is impossible to point out a correct method of fitting a bar shoe, as each new case differs so much from all others. Some smiths cannot make a bar shoe, because they are poor forgers of iron. Such men should not be allowed to tamper with a horse's foot afflicted with ailment, under any circumstances.

In seeking information in books or papers, we often come across the expression, " use a bar shoe." The smith

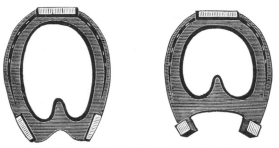

Figs. 132 and 133—Two other Forms of Bar Shoes.

is left in the dark with that short expression. It gives him but an idea, all the rest lies with himself. A bar shoe works some very fine cures occasionally, and it would be a benefit to shoers if a cut and a description of each case of the kind

Figs. 134 and 135—Still Additional Forms of Bar Shoes.

were published. Some smiths pride themselves on making a bar shoe without welding the bar separately. It is just as convenient to weld the bar across if you have a piece of iron at hand suitable. Some blacksmiths place a gum or leather pad over the bar to rest the frog on, and to act as a cushion. Oftentimes this device produces good results. The results of the application of a bar shoe are very uncertain. Some smiths can fit an ordinary shoe with good success, but are totally in darkness when the least judgment or ingenuity is required in the work. In the application and proper fitting of a bar shoe to a horse's foot there is need of great care. There are many floormen who have

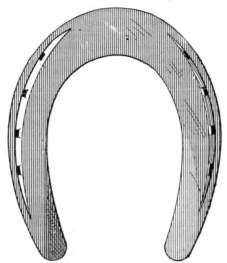

Fig. 136—Showing the Shoe J. F. Button uses on Contracted Feet.

the knack of setting a shoe after it has been fitted by the fireman with better results than if they nailed it when first fitted. In Figs. 131, 132, 133, 134 and 135 are given several forms of bar shoes.—*By* C. S.

Shoeing Contracted Feet.

I herewith explain my method of shoeing horses that have contracted feet.

The hoof should first be well and neatly pared down, all

dead horn removed from the sole and the wall thinned by rasping. I then shoe with a shoe made as shown in the illustration, Fig. 136. I shape the shoe with the inside at the heels the highest. This has the tendency to spread the foot. I leave this shoe on about three weeks, and then re-shoe, using a shoe with a little more spread. After a few re-settings you will have the heel as wide as required.

I have shod a great many horses after this simple method, and never knew it to fail. In this section of the country the ground is very hard and dry, and in consequence the hoofs of horses are apt to get very hard and dry. For such I use the following liniment to soften :

Linseed Oil...4 ozs.
Saltpetre..4 ozs.
Oil of Spike...2 ozs.
Aqua Ammonia...2 ozs.

Soak the entire hoof with this twice a day, and there will be no trouble with hard dry hoofs.—*By* J. F. BUTTON.

Tool for Measuring Angle of Horses' Hoofs.

I have an instrument for measuring the angle of a horse's hoof, which I describe for the benefit of my brother smiths. The tool complete is seen at Fig. 137. Hold the foot in position between the knees, with shoe removed ; place the prongs A, A, level on each quarter, with the toe touching the upright at B; push the upright tight to the wall of the foot in front, tighten the thumb screw C, when you will find the correct angle marked. It will fit any size foot.

The piece A, A, D, is made from a piece $\frac{3}{8}$ x $\frac{1}{8}$ inch split to F. The prongs are drawn to $\frac{1}{8}$ x $\frac{5}{16}$ inch, and perfectly level on top. Make slot hole at B, $1\frac{1}{4}$ x $\frac{5}{16}$ of an inch. Saw a slot, D, in which fasten the quadrant. The upright is made from a piece $\frac{5}{16}$ x $\frac{1}{2}$ inch, $6\frac{1}{2}$ inches long, with slot and set screw at G, to slide over the quadrant, which is made from a piece of steel $\frac{1}{16}$ x $\frac{9}{16}$ inch. The figures are put on with acid. Flow melted beeswax over the quadrant; be careful to have every part well coated,

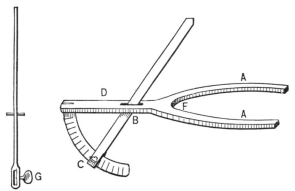

Fig. 137—Tool for Measuring Angle of Horse's Hoofs.

mark the figures through the wax, and cover with sulphuric acid ; it will eat into the metal where the wax has been removed.—*By* D. F. K.

How to Treat Horses' Feet for Corns.

Corns in horses' feet are very often troublesome things that blacksmiths have to contend with in shoeing. The variety and extent of the disease is at times somewhat perplexing, and it is not much wonder that the question is so often asked : "What is the best way to get rid of them?"

In this article it is not the intention to enter into a detailed statement of the various stages of the disease, nor to give methods of treatment that ought to be, or should be pursued by a veterinary surgeon. I will simply indicate a general method that may be adopted at blacksmith or horseshoeing shops.

The causes that lead to corns are various and extensive.

It might be safely said that there is *no* particular cause for corns at all, notwithstandlng the learned opinions and diagnoses of many writers.

It is generally said that the shoes, or shoeing, cause them, when, in fact, it is well known that corns grow in feet that have had, perhaps, only one shoeing—but the blacksmith has often to bear the blame where there ought to be none, and to quietly listen to the inuendo and remote insinuations that are often leveled at him. The writer has often seen feet diseased by corns, when there was no possibility of the shoes having caused them—yet shoeing causes them sometimes, and also proper shoeing can perfect a cure in some cases.

Corns and bruises of the sole are commonly seen in horses' feet, and they are caused in some cases by a general weakness of the foot, in others by an undue pressure of the shoe at a particular point ; or by the shoe being loose and gravel and other substances gathering under it, and thereby being hammered into the sole ; or by a tendency of the foot to contraction, which obviously causes an unnatural pressure on the weaker portions of the foot, thereby causing a squeeze which results in corns or other bruises.

Again, corns will appear in feet when we can hardly account for them, but when they are there we must do what we can to eradicate them. Therefore allow me to advance a general method of treatment that can be pursued in every ordinary case that is usually treated by a horseshoer.

On examining the foot, if it needs paring, pare it down to the customary limit. Then if the corn is of recent origin, pare it out so that the affected parts will be below the level of the other parts of the foot ; fit the shoe so that it will bear evenly and level all around on the outer crust of the foot— keeping it slightly off the sole all around, and particularly at the point where the corn is seated. It is, perhaps, a good idea to lightly cauterize the parts with a small heated rod, and to occasionally apply a little turpentine or good hoof ointment to the affected parts.

Of course this treatment is for *new corns,* but for old and stubborn ones a different course will have to be adopted, which should be about as follows : Pare around and down as deep as you can without injury to the healthy parts of the foot, which you must watch, so that you may not do any unnecesary cutting. After having the diseased parts well cleaned out, pour some turpentine into the cavity and fill with fresh horse manure. This is to keep any foreign matter from entering. Before stopping the cavity you might put in some pine tar and then stop with the manure. Fit the shoe neatly, and if you find it necessary in order to cover the cavity, you can broaden the shoe at that point so that it will cover it, but remember to keep the shoe from pressing at that part. When a foot is badly used up with corns, bruises, and misused from disease or otherwise, it is a very good plan to have the whole surface of the sole covered by a leather covering, under which put some cotton or oakum, saturated with pine tar or some good foot ointment. It will stimulate the foot to a healthy growth and will soften it, which will tend to drive out that hard and bone-like nature which is a great hindrance to the healthy growth of the foot.—*By* I. A. C.

Glycerine for Softening Feet.

I beg to differ with those who believe in the use of cow manure or oil to soften hoofs ; the latter should never be employed and the former very seldom. My objection to cow manure is, that by using it often, the ammonia it contains destroys the frog and produces thrush and hoof-rot. My objection to oils, tar, etc., is that they render the hoof brittle, and loosen the nails. The best thing that I have found is to have the owners of horses soak the horse's feet occasionally in cold water, and every few days apply glycerine to the coronary ring, rubbing it in well, especially in dry weather. I know from experience, that glycerine will soften and toughen the hoof. The difference between tar and oil and glycerine is that the two former close the pores and keep out water, while glycerine will mix with water, which I have found in my practice to be the best for horses' feet.

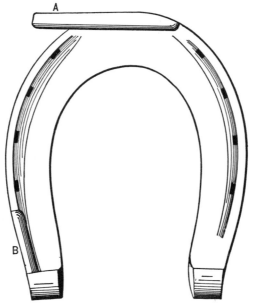

Fig. 138—A Shoe for Draught Horses.

I do not think I know all about horseshoeing, by any means, notwithstanding I have run a shop for quite a number of years. I am learning and expect to continue to learn something every day.—*By* RAB OF THE WYNDE.

Two Improved Horseshoes.

If a draught horse pulls from the outside toe, the outside quarter will wire, and to overcome this tendency I have de-

signed the shoe shown in Fig. 138.   The device may be applied to any ordinary shoe in the following manner :   Weld
the toe piece *A* on the shoe, making the piece extend over
the outside rim of the shoe from half an inch to one inch.
Then stave up the outside heel of the shoe sufficiently to get a

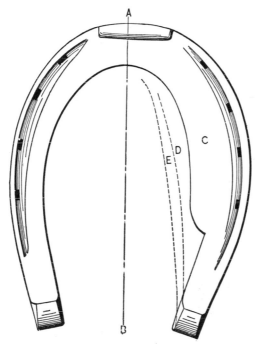

Fig. 139--A Side-Weight Shoe.

good, broad covering for the narrowed heels and quarters.
Use the round fulling tool to swedge the shoe, and swedge
wide enough to get a good bar pressure.   Turn up the
heels, weld a calk on the outside heels and fit the shoe snug
to the wall, up to both sides of the frog. The effect of the
projecting toe piece is to brace or stay the weak part of

the ankle and foot. After two or three shoeings the foot will regain its natural movements. Fig. 138 represents the shoe as designed for draught horses. Fig. 139 is a side weight shoe for improving the action behind. I use the shoe also for some cases of interfering.

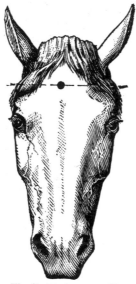

Fig. 40—How to Kill a Horse.

In the engraving *A B* denote a line dividing the foot. *C* is the outside or weighted side of the shoe. *D* and *E* indicate the degrees to which weight may be added in the web. When the shoe requires additional weight to carry the foot out, this weight may be added in the web up to the line *D*, and if more weight is needed increase the web toward *E*. I have used this shoe for ten years with good results.— *By* G. E. R.

How to Kill a Horse.

Though the horse is one of man's most faithful servants,

it sometimes becomes advisable, for the servant's own good, that the master should turn executioner.

It is not a pleasant task the man then finds before him.

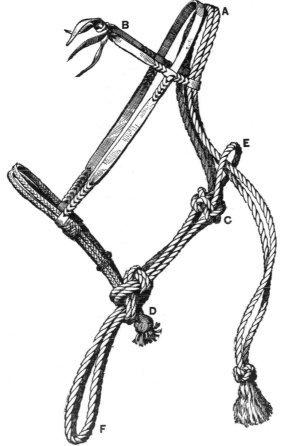

Fig. 141—A Cowboy Halter. Showing the Bands, Knots, Loop and Latch.

It is not one that most men know how to properly perform.

Through the nervousness or inability of the executioner numbers of the poor animals are needlessly tortured when it becomes necessary to put them to death. The American Society for Prevention of Cruelty to Animals has formulated the following rules :

First.—Shoot with a 32-caliber or larger pistol, at the point indicated by a dot in Fig. 140, placing the muzzle within a few inches of the head.

Second.—Aim four or five inches above the head.

Third.—Be careful not to shoot too low.

Fig. 142—The Theodore Knot Shown at C in Fig. 141.

Cowboy Halter.

In this connection is illustrated one of those marvelous productions of the wild West, a cowboy halter. The artist has succeeded in very fully portraying the appearance of this remarkable piece of harness, even to the wonderful knots which it contains.

In adjusting the halter the rope at the point *A*, Fig. 141, goes back of the ears. *B* is the brow band in front of the ears, and is always made of light leather, as there is no strain on it. *C* is perhaps, all things considered, the most remarkable knot ever tied. There are only a few people, it is said, in the West even, who understand its intricacies. It is called the "Theodore knot," and is said to be tied without ends to work with. This knot is shown enlarged and loosened in Fig. 142, so as to give our readers a chance, if possible, to trace the different strands composing

Fig. 143—First Step in Tying the Theodore Knot.

it. The artist has shaded each rope differently, solely for the purpose of showing as near as possible how the knot is

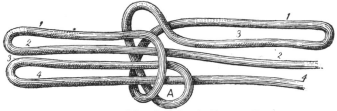

Fig. 144—Second Step in Tying the Theodore Knot.

tied. Of course practically all the ropes are alike. The halter before us is made of quarter-inch rope. D is what is

Fig. 145—Third Step in Tying the Theodore Knot.

called a "Turk's Head," or Hackamore knot, and is also more or less complicated and difficult to understand. E represents the throat latch. F is the loop to which the lariat is attached.

The Theodore Knot.

I will try and explain how I tie the Theodore knot used on the Cowboy Halter.

First, you take a rope and double it twice so as to have four strands. Then take the strand No. 1 in Fig. 143 and wind it around the others as shown. Then take strand No. 3 and double it around as shown in Fig. 144; hold the strands with your fingers so they will not slip, until you get them all in place. Then take strand No. 2 and double it around as shown in Fig. 145 and stick the end through the loop *A* made with strand No. 3. Next take strand No.

Fig. 146--The Theodore Knot Complete.

4 and double it around as shown in Fig. 146, and put the end through the loops *B* and *C* made with strands 3 and 1. When you have finished this, pull all the strands together and draw the knot tight, because if you pull one strand harder than another it will pull the knot out of shape. From this explanation I think almost anybody will be able to tie the knot. I don't think it can be tied without putting the ends through the two last used strands, Nos. 2 and 4. Therefore be sure and place the two strands that are used first, Nos. 1 and 3, first and third, because they have no ends. If, as claimed by some it could be tied without ends, it would come untied.—*By* W. K. HIGGIN.

CHAPTER XI.

DOCKING.

The Process of Docking Described and Illustrated—Is the Process a Cruel One?—Objections and Advantages— New York Fashion.

To dock, or not to dock, that is the question. Whether 'tis nobler in the mind to suffer the slings and arrows of outrageous fashion, by not having your horse's tail docked or to take up arms against a sea of troubles, liable to be heaped upon you by the Massachusetts society with the long name, if you conform to the modes of the day in respect to your horse.

As nearly every one who owns a horse is well aware, it is the "fad" nowadays to drive, ride on, or ride behind, a horse with a docked tail. Webster says to dock is to cut off, as the end of a thing, to cut short, to curtail, to clip; and that is just what is done to the tail of a horse that is afterward said to be "docked."

Years ago, before it was found necessary to organize societies to suppress and prevent cruelty to animals, the simple act of docking a horse's tail was not considered even of enough consequence to cause a passing note or comment, but in these days of progressive ideas things are different.

The man who docks horses' tails says he subjects the horse to little or no pain or inconvenience afterward, and he satisfies the craving of public taste for things that are fashionable as well as beautiful.

The word having been given that the surgeon was ready to dock the horse, bandages were put around the horse's hind fetlocks and lower legs. Around the bandages a leather strap at the end of a long rope was placed, the other end of the rope being tied about the horse's neck, and resting on

Fig. 147--Cauterizing Tool.

the breast. " This," said the operator, " is done to prevent accident caused by the horse kicking, but it is not a necessity." At the horse's head stood a man with twisters about the horse's nose, which he tightened only slightly. The

Ftg. 148—Docking Machine.

horse being now tied, and in a vise, so to speak, so that he could do no damage, a strong cord was twisted and tied on his tail about half an inch above where the horse's owner desired to have the tail docked. The operator explained that

Fig. 149—The Pricking Knife.

this binding was done to prevent the flow of blood from the tail after the cutting. The rope being bound tightly about the tail, the operator brought into requisition a queer-looking machine, Fig. 148, made very much after the style of a lemon squeezer. On the upper portion of the "squeezer," near the end where the two pieces of wood connected, was a semi-circular bladed knife, and on the lower portion a bed in which the knife rested when the machine closed up. The operator got the horse's tail between the handles of this machine as shown in the accompanying illustration, Fig. 152, and in a jiffy the knife closed down on the tail and a portion dropped to the floor. As the knife penetrated the member the horse winced for a moment, but after the member was severed he did not seem to suffer. The next portion of the operation was the singeing or cauterizing of the end of the tail that remained on the horse. A singeing iron, Fig. 147,

Fig. 150--The Flag-Tail Horse, after Docking and Pricking.

white with heat, resembling in every respect a common carriage nut wrench, with a small hole in one end, was brought into use. While the "docker" moved this iron over the raw part of the tail the horse again showed signs of pain, but his actions were not violent enough to disturb in the least the man working the hot iron, who very complacently puffed the cigar in his mouth and attended strictly to business without saying a word. In less than two minutes from the time the horse was hitched the entire process of docking was over, all the fixtures about the horse to keep him quiet were removed, and the dumb beast with the new-fangled and fashionable tail had his nose stuck in his hay rack pulling down hay to eat, little thinking what a great change a moment had made in his appearance, and what a want he filled for the wealthy gentleman who desired to be in the fashion.

The practice of docking, as it is at present done, is not in the least cruel, for the cutting off of the tail is almost instantaneous. The tail is cut straight across between the bones nowadays, and not as it used to be cut in docking a few years ago. Then the tail was cut V-shape and the edges were sewed together and allowed to heal. It took

Fig. 151--A Short Dock.

some time for healing, and the lower end of the appendage was sore till the part healed entirely. Now every particle of soreness ends with the cauterizing of the part cut.

Docking and pricking a horse's tail makes the horse hold his tail almost straight up in the air as shown in the accompanying cut, Fig. 150. Docking a horse to conform to the present fashion makes him hold the stub of his tail almost straight out from his body, and that in itself is not cruel, and can hardly come under the head of crime, insomuch as the hair in the tail is almost as long after the end

Fig. 152—In the Act of " Docking."

of the tail is cut off as before the docking is done. To make the tail conform to the present fashion, the hair must be cut off up to within a foot or so of the root; and then again, this practice is hardly any more cruel than the simple banging of a horse's tail, without docking, and banging is an every-day occurrence. The pricking is done after the docking is finished. A pricking blade (a cut of which is shown here-with, Fig. 149), is run into the horse's tail at one side and then the other in two or three parts. Then the "pricker" draws the knife towards the outer end of the tail, cutting

Fig. 153--Banged Tail Cob.

all the muscles and tissues on its path. Once cut, the tail is drawn up and hitched with a pulley block in the position the owner desires the horse to carry his appendage, and in that position it is held till all the cuts made in the operation are healed.

After this operation is performed, the hair in the tail is cut to suit the fashionable tastes. If the old-fashioned "flag" tail is desired—that is to say, such a tail as Flora Temple had—the hair in the tail is close trimmed on the sides, combed flat and parted on top. If only the ordinary dock is wanted, the hair in the tail is cut off in bang fashion without other trimming. If some other style is wanted, the man with shears must make that style, for the veterinary's part of the fashion ends with the docking and pricking.

The fashion in New York is to put a long dock, with square or fan ends, on a heavy brougham horse. To secure the proper effect on a tail of this nature, there must be an ample supply of long hair before the docking is done. A long bang is the favorite style of tail for the saddle horse, and when properly trimmed it becomes a desirable style for the the coach horse. It is said to be the most abused of any style, as stablemen who want to imitate fashion, and at the same time rid themselves of much trouble in cleaning and combing, can clip the hair without removing the tail.

A long, heavy tail is the fashion on heavy, slow-moving, high-stepping coach horses, while the "pancake," which is short, but, instead of being cut square, is trimmed to hang with rounded ends, is a style for riding to saddle or in a two-wheeler.

What are known as cob horses are the kind of horses generally docked. In the language of a stableman, a cob is a little horse, big at both ends. By that is meant a full made horse that is not too large for carriage or family use. Cobs come from all sections of the country, and are of no particular breed. They bring a much larger price with docked tails than without. Docking is an "English" fashion, and that is why it is now so popular in America. It is sometimes desirable to dock a horse to cure him of ugliness and kicking, but fully ninety-nine of every one hundred horses docked have their tails cut off because their owners want to live up the fashion of the times.—*Boston Herald.*

CHAPTER XII.

TIPS FOR TROTTERS.

This Method Growing in Favor—Diseased Feet Cured by the New Method—The Simpson Tip—Toe Weights and Tip Combined.

Among the problems which have engaged the attention of horsemen the world over is how best to protect the equine foot, and at the same time interfere in the least possible way with the natural condition of that valuable member. In America, where the harness horse has been brought nearer to perfection in grit and speed than anywhere else, the subject of shoeing has been carefully studied, and, as a result, many of the difficulties arising from old-time methods have been successfully overcome. From the heavy draught horse to the fast roadster or racing trotter, there has been a general improvement in the fashioning and appliance of footgear, so that to-day there is a vast difference between the crude mass of iron used by the Arabs and Moors in the middle ages and the neatly turned pieces of steel or iron forged by the expert horseshoers of the United States.

Since races came in vogue the care of the animal's foot has been more closely studied than when the horse was simply a beast of burden, and the famous drivers of the last quarter of a century have achieved much of their success by giving special attention to shoeing the flyers they trained and drove. The late Dan Mace, whose pre-eminence as a reinsman earned him the soubriquet of the Wizard of the Sulkey, was one of the first professional drivers to make a close study of this subject, and his quick perception enabled him to see where many evils resulting from old methods of making and nailing on the shoe could be remedied. He was the first prominent driver to apply toe weights, whose use has done much to correct imperfections in the gait of the trotter and enabled Maud S. to attain to the unparalleled speed of a mile in 2:08¾. Other famous whips, such as Hickok, of California ; Doble, of Chicago ; Murphy, of New York ; Goldsmith, of Orange County, and John Splan, of everywhere, have followed in Mace's footsteps and included shoeing in the curriculum of their professional course.

But with all the improvement, the vise-like character of

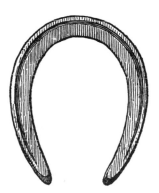

Fig. 152—Modern Model Shoe.

the orthodox shoe remains, a sample of which is shown in Fig. 152 and many a promising trotter has broken down when on the threshold of a brilliant career by reason of his inability to wear the iron band which has been considered indispensable to his education and development.

Even those who have not given the subject any consider_ ation can see at a glance that the immovable piece of metal on the horse's foot hinders the natural growth of the outer shell or wall which covers and protects the delicate mechan-

ism that enables the animal to attain his flight of speed.
This cramping of the wall or crust brings about numerous
diseases, the most prevalent of which is that known as contraction, of which an example is shown in Fig. 153. This
the reader may compare with the healthy foot shown in
Fig. 154. In its natural state the horse's foot is nearly
round and slightly wider than it is long. Shoeing has the
effect of changing this natural shape by elongating the hoof
and by keeping the heel from spreading, causing the contraction above referred to, the *bete noir* of every horseman
and the chief enemy of every horse that has worn shoes.

Other common ailments from the same cause are corns,

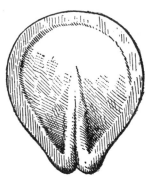

Fig. 153—Bad Case of Contraction.

produced by the pressure on the heel, and quarter cracks,
which result from the bursting or splitting of the wall of
the foot owing to the unusual thinness of the horn, which
being bound by the shoe is not strong enough to withstand
the pressure from within.

It is claimed by many practical horsemen that a radical
remedy has been found for these and kindred diseases that
come from the stereotyped method of shoeing. This is the
use of what are known as tips, which are nothing more

than shoes without heels. Tips in a crude form have been in use for a long time, and were probably employed as a protection to horses that were turned out to graze, and designed to prevent the front of the hoof from breaking off in the pasture. The wild horse is constantly on the move, and the hoof is thus worn down proportionate to its growth, but the domesticated animal is less active and even unbroken colts require to be looked after to see that the feet do not grow too long. Close observers found that when a horse had become so crippled from shoeing that he could no longer be driven, the quickest remedy was to remove the shoes, tack on a light plate or tip, and give the animal a rest. Nature soon worked a cure when there was no iron band to cramp the contracted heel, and the horse was restored to usefulness. Further experiment showed that these tips could be utilized for every-day wear when the horse was in harness, and with good results. Gradually the use of tips has been tested and investigated, until to-day there are many horsemen who have discarded the old-time shoe entirely, and use nothing but tips.

For racing purposes the tip has also been tested, and with results claimed to be satisfactory. Joseph Cairn Simpson, editor of the San Francisco *Breeder and Sportsman,* is the acknowledged pioneer in adapting tips to the trotting race horse. Mr. Simpson is a veteran breeder and trainer of trotters, and in common with his fellow turfmen used the regulation shoe covering the foot to the heel. Some years ago his attention was attracted to the use of tips, and he began to experiment with them on his own horses, both runners and trotters. The results of his investigations, extending over a period of about fifteen years, is told in a book published by Mr. Simpson entitled "Tips and Toe Weights." The most notable instances of Mr. Simpson's success with tips are the turf performances of the two stallions, Anteeo and Antevolo, bred by him from Elec-

tioneer, out of his mare Columbine, by A. W. Richmond,
dam Columbia, by the famous thoroughbred racer Bonnie
Scotland.   Both Anteeo and Antevolo were shod with tips,
as in Fig. 155, as colts, and their entire development and
training were conducted with no other protection for their
feet.   In 1885 Mr. Simpson's efforts were crowned with two
fast performances by the horses, when Anteeo, then six
years old, trotted a mile in 2:16¼, and Antevolo made a
record of 2:19¼ in his four-year-old form.

One of the most valuble results of Mr. Simpson's investigations was the improvement made by him in the application of the tip.   At first it was placed on the foot, like the
shoe, and tapered or feathered to a point to keep the hoof
as level as possible.   In this form the healthy growth of
the frog and natural shape of the foot were retained, but
it was almost impossible to balance the horse properly,
and there was an undue strain on the tendons.   Mr. Simpson tells how he got over this drawback to his pet hobby,
as follows : " I made the tip of nearly a uniform thickness,
a majority of them having a .quarter of an inch of metal,
which was filed square.   A shoulder was cut in the wall,
and so much of the sole as the width of the web required
and all back of the shoulder was left full and rounded with
a file to protect the edge."

Since the first adoption of this method of letting in the
tip till it is level with the uncovered part of the foot there
has been another improvement, namely, the cutting of the
ends to a point, or diagonally, as shown in Fig. 156.

" In the Spring of 1886," said Mr. E. T. Bedford, of the
Thompson & Bedford Co., to a reporter of the *Sun* recently,
" I purchased the chestnut mare Kitty Patchen, by Job
Stuart.   She had won several races, and in 1884 made a
record at Boston of 2:21¼.   In 1885 the mare was campaigned
again, but with no success, owing to the bad condition of
her feet.   Her trainer, A. J. Feek, of Syracuse, said she had

bruised her heel, and she was then shod with the ordinary shoe, with a pad and sponge between the shoe and foot.

"When I purchased Kitty Patchen," continued Mr. Bedford, "her feet were in a terrible condition. What with the fever produced by contraction and the result of constant soaking, her hoofs were so brittle that they could be broken with the finger and thumb, and the mare suffered with corns and stood with her feet forward in an unnatural position. At first I had her shod with bar shoes, which relieved the corns temporarily by removing the pressure.

Fig. 154—Sole of a Healthy Foot.

As the hoof grew out the trouble returned, and I resolved to try what the use of tips would do. I followed Mr. Simpson's instructions, and Kitty found instant relief ; the corns disappeared, the hoof resumed its natural consistency, and instead of a cripple I soon had a trotter free from lameness. To-day the mare has as good feet as any horse in my stable, and I believe she can go faster than when she was on the turf. Late last Fall, on election day, in fact, I drove her half a mile to wagon in 1:11½ and a mile to a road cart in 2:24¼. With a lighter driver, but over regulation weight, she trotted a mile to sulkey in 2:21¾, which is within half a second of her best race record, and that with no preparation. These trials were all done in tips, and at Norwalk, Conn., in 1886, Kitty trotted publicly in 2:26½, winning a five-heat race."

" Wherein do you think tips are chiefly to be preferred to shoes?" was asked.

" Because they give a horse the use of the whole foot," replied Mr. Bedford, "sole, frog and horn, thus enabling the natural elasticity to be fully exerted. I believe they tend to make a horse trot more squarely and keep the gait natural. I know that in Kitty Patchen's case boots were discarded after she was shod with tips, and her gait improved visibly."

" Would you do away entirely with the regulation shoe?"

" Most assuredly. My own experience convinces me that for trotters and roadsters tips are the thing. I drive my horses over all kinds of roads, and their feet keep in perfect condition. I have observed, also, that many draught horses in New York and Brooklyn wear tips, and they are noticeable for the good condition of their feet. If you will examine the horses used by the Havemeyer Sugar Refinery, for instance, you will see that they do their heavy work in tips."

Among the smiths of the metropolis that make and nail shoes on fine road horses and trotters George Staples is probably the most famous. Staples is a New Englander, who was for many years the foreman of Dan Mace's well-known shop on upper Broadway. Though now in his seventy-fifth year, Staples continues actively at work and has charge of an establishment on Fifty-eighth street, near Broadway. This veteran knight of the forge has shod some of the famous trotters, living and dead, and looked after Maud S.'s feet when W. H. Vanderbilt owned her.

When asked his opinion of tips, Mr. Staples said : " They are a very good thing, but few people know anything about

them. No, I don't shoe many of the trotters that come here
with tips. I know of one or two that use them. Yes, the
old style of shoe causes contracted feet, corns and other
troubles. I can manage corns quite easily, if the horse
comes regularly, by cutting away the heel slightly to take
off the pressure. For contracted feet I use a spring,
invented by Mr. Mace, to expand the heel, and this helps to
keep the foot in its natural condition. I scarcely think tips
will supersede shoes, for they do not suit all kinds of feet,
in my opinion."

Mr. Staples then selected a shoe that had been used on

Fig. 155—The Simpson Tip Set on the Foot.

the forward foot of a fast trotter, from which the cut used
to illustrate the modern style of shoe is made.

" You will notice," he remarked, " that there has been a
great improvement in making shoes of late years. Instead
of the great load of iron that was once the regulation style,
the shoe is much lighter, and steel is greatly used nowadays. Then, again, we do not cut the foot down, as formerly, but the sole and frog are left in a natural condition.
I suppose in some parts of the country they adhere to old
methods yet, but here in New York we have learned by

experience to interfere as little as possible with the natural condition of the foot."

An inquiry at some of the large boarding stables near the Park showed that here and there tips have been used with satisfactory results, especially where a horse has been made lame by the full-length shoe. John J. Quinn, 124th street, near Seventh avenue, said that he had used tips on trotters with success, but he did not think they would do for steady driving on the rough avenues.

"The fast mare Old Maid, who trotted at Fleetwood in

Fig. 156—Antevolo's Tip.

2:21¾ some four years ago, on a wager to beat 2:22 was shod with tips," said Mr. Quinn, " and I think Johnny Murphy has used them on some of the horses he has trained."

D. B. Herrington, manager of the Hudson River Driving Park and stock farm owned by Jacob Ruppert, at Poughkeepsie, was in the city recently, and when asked what he thought of using tips for racing replied: "I have not given them a sufficient trial to test their use in a race, but I have tried them with good results as a cure for corns and quarter cracks. Some years ago I used those with ends drawn out or tapered to a point, but have not tried those set in the hoof after the Simpson method."

W. C. Trimble, of Newburg, is one of the best known of the old-time trainers in the East and has had many successful campaigners through the summer circuit. He, too, has been experimenting with tips, and has become a strong advocate of their use. He first used them on a big bay gelding named Jim Brooker, who had made a record of 2:44¾ in 1885 and had afterward broken down from terrible quarter cracks that developed whenever he was put in training. The horse was sent to Mr. Trimble, who substituted tips for the troublesome shoes, and the trotter's feet healed up in a wonderfully short time. The veteran turfite considers tips a valuable boon to the horse suffering from ailments caused by wearing shoes.

A notable instance where tips are worn by a modern star

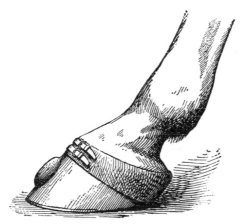

Fig. 157—Toe-Weight and Tip Combined.

of the trotting turf is that of the gray gelding Jack, 2:19¾, the Chicago crack that stood at the head of the Grand Circuit winners for 1888. Jack is remarkably pure gaited and could be barefooted if necessary. Budd Doble used tips of about four ounces weight on Jack in his races last year, and the horse kept improving all the time, gradually lowering his record from Cleveland to New York, where he made his fastest mark in the Fleetwood Stake.

In the book published by Joseph Cairn Simpson he advocates the doing away of the old method of weighting the trotter to balance him by adding to the shoe, and claims that better results can be obtained by the use of the toe weight in conjunction with the tip, as shown in Fig. 157. It is contended by turf men that one ounce of weight on the toe is equivalent to from one and a half to three ounces on the sole of the foot, though some trotters will not go level or fast with toe weights, and must be balanced by weight in the shoe or distributed about the foot in leather weight pockets. Others require the toe weights, which give the balancing medium in the smallest compass.

As yet the use of tips is naturally looked on with conservatism by many horsemen, and like all other innovations it continues to be subjected to criticism and open opposition. In the face of the undeniable fact that there has been comparatively little advance made in the general method of shoeing, and valuable horses are still ruined by unskillful and ignorant smiths, any plan that will obviate the present difficulties deserves a full and impartial trial. The question as to the utility of tips for racing purposes is really a secondary one compared with the greater benefit that will follow any plan whereby the carriage and draught horse may be kept freer from the numerous disabilities of foot and limb which continue to be a serious drawback to their commercial value and term of usefulness.—*N. Y. Sun.*

CHAPTER XIII.

HORSE PHYSIOGNOMY.

An Ingenious Theory of Mind Reading Applied to Many Conspicuous Race Track Favorites—Peculiarities of the Features Which Correspond with Well-Known Qualities of the Horse.

"Horses are so much like men," said a shrewd Union Club man the other day, "that many of the proverbs made for their riders apply equally well to the nags, and even the general laws of physiognomy may be studied out in a stable with results almost as satisfactory as they would be in a drawing-room. You can tell—or most people think they can, at least—the character of a man by looking at his face. I believe a practised eye can learn from the study of a racer's head what the character of his pace will be. It might even come to pass that a study of the heads of the contesting beasts would enable an expert to pick out the winner beforehand. Certain I am, at all events, that a horse's character is generally written in his features as indelibly as is a man's."

There is a venerable superstition that the front view of the average horse's head presents to the eye, not averse to seeing it, the general outlines of a coffin. The idea is, of course, purely fanciful. Much, however, may be learned from the study of the equine features as shown in the accompanying cut, Fig. 158. Glancing at the dimensions indicated by the dotted lines $A\ldots B$, $C\ldots D$, $E\ldots F$ and I

....J, the horseman reads the character of his beast. Suppose this reader of the equine mind wanders into a famous stable the day before the Derby—a stable containing several probable or at least possible winners. The horses, eight or ten of them, perhaps, have their heads out of the stalls and regard the new comer with languid interest. He sees a horse whose head is short from the eyes to the ears, between the lines A....B and E....F. There is a slight concavity of the skull where the line C....D crosses it. E....F is not

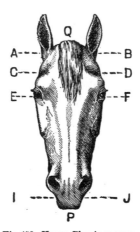

Fig. 158—Horse Physiognomy.

as wide as it might be. The equine mind-reader can't tell yet whether his subject hasn't both strength and speed. But he knows almost to a certainty that he hasn't much sense and is probably deficient in courage and energy.

Going to the next stall he sees a nag whose mouth is large and flabby-looking, the line I....J being of goodly length, while the nostrils, on the contrary, are small and apparently inelastic. C....D and E....F may be generous in dimensions, but the small nostril is a bad sign for staying qualities.   The horse can't get his wind in the heat of a terrific struggle without big, wide, sensitive nostrils.   The big heart to pump the air in and the big lungs to hold it—for it is a question how much of a supply of " wind " the animal must keep on hand during a race and how far nature permits him to renew it—are of no avail without the wide nostrils to gather it.

The next head that greets him with a whinny, a bright eye and a docile face is turned half sideways, as in Fig. 159.

Fig. 159—Great Breadth of Jaw.

The breadth of the jaw $L....N$ is shown to be great.   The equine reader knows that he has strength and perhaps speed there.   So he pursues his investigations, and at the close of the jaunt through this stable he may have mentally decided that three horses out of the ten are probably safe to bet on.

But there are a great many horsemen who deny that accurate judgments can be formed in this way.   Whether judgments so formed are safe to tie to, especially to tie money to, is a new and an interesting question.   Should the racing season see it develop as it promises, it is not improbable that amateur equine readers will be found as thick as flies along Broadway, stopping draymen to inquire if their animals are wide across the face, examining the brain bumps of beer horses and the eyes of carriage teams.

Fig. 160 is a portrait of Eurus, drawn from life. Proctor Knott is shown in Fig. 161.

In order to appreciate Eurus he must be seen in his stall as well as with his blinkers on, charging along the track

Fig. 160—Head of Eurus.

with that deviltry which equine readers say the above picture brings out in the ears and eyes and general expression. Looking at him carefully it is seen that his face is slightly "dished" below the eyes, and his nose has a round, Roman turn. His jaw is big and wide and, recurring to Fig. 158 Eurus is found to be wide along the line $E....F$ and big at $C....D$. He is, beyond a doubt, one of the most interesting horses on the American turf. It is never safe to bet heavily against him in a race in which he is entered.

There is no knowing what he may do. His brain box, measured by $C....D$, is very roomy. Eurus undoubtedly reasons. His temper is notorious. He is docile enough except on the track. "A lady could drive him." But in a race he swerves and does very much as he chooses. It runs ir the breed sometimes for a horse to act that way on the track.

"Eurus runs best on a muddy track," it is often said.

Fig. 161—Head of Proctor Knott.

But none of the equine mind-readers profess to be able to tell that from looking at him. It is experience only that proves a horse to be good on the mud. That doesn't show in his features, but it shows in his action and in the actual record of what he has done.

Looking at Proctor Knott's picture no indication of the lack of "heart" or courage, or perseverance is seen. Proctor Knott is a coarse, ragged-looking plebeian of a horse. His head is unquestionably ugly, when compared

with even that of Eurus, whose expression is scarcely com-
patible with beauty.   Compared with the Bard of Hanover,
Proctor Knott's "plainness" becomes absolutely plain.
His color is a mealy chestnut.   The broad blaze widening out
over his nose does not enhance his looks.   He is not wide
across the eyes on the line $E \ldots F$ (see Fig. 158), nor is his
brain pan, shown by $C \ldots D$, to be capacious.

Reading a horse's character from his head is like trying
to read a man's character from his face.   Nine times

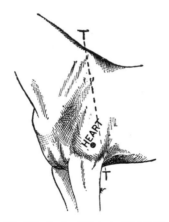

Fig. 162—Angle of Body and Forelegs.

out of ten it may be all right.   The other and tenth time it
may be so widely and utterly wrong as to upset the entire
theory.   But it's the same way with men.   When a crime
requires intellect, skill and discretion for its execution it
doesn't necessarily brand "criminal" on the man who does
it.   It's your brute crimes which so unmistakably stamp their
impression on their perpetrators.   All signs fail in dry weather.   But you want your horse to have big nostrils and to
be wide between the eyes.   There is no doubt of that.

And of course you want him to "fork close."   The angle,

as shown in Fig. 162, between the forelegs where they join the body must be acute. And you want a long reach from the hip down, a good second thigh, good muscles, and a good lower bone.

King Thomas is shown in Fig. 163, in all his untried splendor. He is the costliest yearling known to the American turf. When sold at Madison Square Garden by Mr. J. B. Haggin, King Thomas was bought for $38,000 by

Fig. 163—King Thomas.

" Lew " Appleby. In twenty-four hours Senator Hearst, who bid against Appleby at the auction, bought King Thomas for $40,000. He has never run yet, and nobody knows what he can do. As shown by the artist, King Thomas has a small head for his size—he is 16.1 hands high and is rather narrow between the eyes. The general effect of his countenance warrants his being called "hatchet-faced." His nose is slightly Roman. He has a powerful chest and shoulders, and his length from hip to whirlbone (see Fig. 164) is good.   King Thomas is a little bit "peaked behind," across the line of $Z....Z$ (Fig. 164).

Close by his famous kinsman in the Chesterbrook Stable, the student of equine nature finds Eurocrydon, full brother of Eurus. Eurocrydon is a large bay colt, evenly turned, with no dimensions indicating any very great power. Eurocrydon hasn't Eurus' brain width or his broad forehead. He has a big mouth and large nostrils. His head is bigger than that of Eurus, and he has the rather remarkably uninteresting habit of sucking his tongue. The breed doesn't show facially in Eurocrydon.

The Bard, shown in Fig. 165, has a strong neck and great

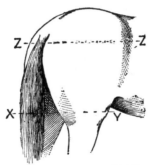

Fig. 164—Showing Hip and Whirlbone.

breadth of jaw, which is shown not only in the portrait, but also along the line $L....N$ in Fig. 159. The Bard, as shown by his face, has a quiet disposition and a good temper. Some people remember Eurus and say "only a fool horse will really run his best in a race after all." It is a problem worth studying whether Eurus doesn't reason it out that he will get just as much oats at night whether he runs or no. So the rogue no doubt thinks it out and concludes that it is just as safe for him to do as he pleases and a great deal funnier. But there is none of this rogue

reasoning in The Bard's face.   His head is small and his
mouth is so dainty that he could almost drink out of a pint
cup.   His head is short, and the brain measure across C....
D (see Fig. 158) is not so great as in Eurus.   Across the line
E....F, between the eyes, the Bard's head is very wide,
and his eyes are big, brown and gentle.   The Bard's leg is
his great beauty.   His hind leg is one of the finest known.
It is as thin as one's hand and as solid and heavy as ivory.
There is no porosity or weakness about it.   The depth

Fig. 165—The Bard.

through the chest on the line T....T (Fig. 162), is very great
in the Bard.

The creature is deceptive in appearance.   He has to be
analyzed for his fine points to be appreciated.   He has both
bottom and speed.   He is tall to the point of legginess and
unusually short from shoulder to cropper.   Eurus has very
broad quarters from hip bone to whirlbone, the Bard only
medium.   Most people like a broad quarter for a horse.
Some good horses are broad behind and others are large

and peaked behind.   When a horse is both short and peaked
behind he isn't to be depended on, many experts agree.
Nor, as far as that goes, is he to be depended on unless you
can lay your three fingers between his eyes.   The Bard is
notably narrow across the lines $Z....Z$ (see Fig. 164), and
remarkably broad in the stifles along the line $X....Y.$ Eurus is very deep from the eye line $E....F$ to the ear line A
$....B$ (see Fig. 158.)   The hollows over a horse's eyes are

Fig. 166—Head of Hanover.

natural and mean nothing in particular, though to an amateur they often give a wrong impression that there is something the matter with the animal. Of course a horse shouldn't
have such deep hollows that you could carry his feed in
them.   And while his neck should be muscular there
shouldn't be an ounce of superfluous flesh on it.   One thing
is certain : if a horse doesn't look symmetrical to the expert
eye the chances are that he isn't all he ought to be.

Hanover, the great Hanover, who has won more money

than any three-year-old that ever started, is seen in Fig. 166, and presents another distinctly interesting type of horse physiognomy. Hanover has won seventeen races in succession. He is five years old and a brave, handsome creature. He went lame last year and a small portion of the nerve was removed from his leg. It was feared this might impair his powers, but it did not. Hanover is of a high equine type; he is wide between the eyes and shows quality in his face, which is decidedly intelligent. His eye is full and big, his nose is straight, his muzzle is small, and the broad blaze on his face does not detract from the general high-bred look of his head. He is over 16 hands high, and has long white stockings. His queer fashion of wagging his head from side to side as he runs has made him widely known on the track.—*N. Y. Sunday World.*

CHAPTER XIV.

OX SHOEING.

Making and Fitting Ox Shoes.

I will give you my ideas on ox shoeing. The first point to be considered is the shoes, that is, which is the cheapest and best, machine or hand-made shoes? There are several companies that make ox shoes. A malleable iron shoe is very good and cheap, but they will not fit all kinds of feet, especially the hind ones. These are not so rounded as the front feet, and should not be so wide in the web.

My idea of the best ox shoe is a hand-made one. It will give the best satisfaction to both parties. · To be sure hand-made shoes cost a little more than machine-made ones, but you can make them at odd times, making some of them more and others less rounded at the toe or heel or both. Then by having a stock on hand you will find shoes that will fit all kinds of feet, thereby saving enough time in putting them on to make up for the extra cost. I take the best refined iron, $1\frac{1}{4}$ inches by $\frac{5}{16}$ inch, for hind shoes, and $1\frac{1}{2}$ inches to $1\frac{3}{4}$ inches by $\frac{5}{16}$ inch for front shoes. I shoulder down and draw out the toe, then shoulder the heel the opposite way, bend over the horn to the desired circle, draw the inside edge thin, and punch the holes with a counter-sink punch so that the nail heads will fit. I like punching better than creasing, as it makes a stronger shoe, and one that will stay in place longer, because the strain comes on the head of the nail, instead of under it, as in most creased shoes.

In fitting up the shoes I turn up the toe and heel, making

a short calk, and punch the holes slanting out, which has a
tendency to make the inside of the shoe lie down on the
bottom of the foot. I like six nail holes in the front shoes
fitted for No. 5 nails; for very large oxen I use No. 6.

In putting shoes on, the foot should be made perfectly
level with a rasp, having each claw on the foot the same
height. When the feet are worn very thin and rounding the
shoe should be fitted carefully to the feet. Always have
the shoe fit the outside wall and circle of the foot. A shoe

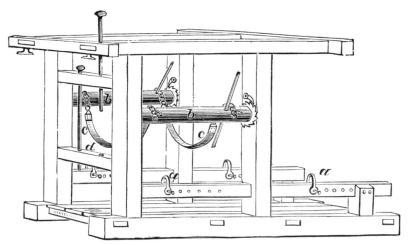

Fig. 167—Frame for Shoeing Oxen.   Scale one-fourth inch.

may be a little short at the toe without serious damage en-
suing, but it should be as long as the foot at the heel and
wide enough in the web to protect the bottom from injury.

In nailing on, start your nail at the inside of the wall and
do not go too high. Care should be taken to avoid drawing
the clinches too hard. Then with a V-shaped tool, cut in
for the clinch and set into place. File the clinch only, as the
shoe should fit the foot; do not file the foot to fit the shoe.
—*By "* OX SHOES.*"*

Frame, for Shoeing Oxen.

I have shod oxen for thirty-four years, and think I can
lay claim to some experience.   Herewith I send you a draft
of my ox frame, Fig. 167.   The sills of the frame are of pine,
10 inches square and 12 feet long; posts, 8 inches square;
foot and neck beams the same size; plates and cross-plates,
6 x 8; foot rest, 3 x 6, hard wood; diameter of rollers, 5
inches, and they are made of hard wood; stanchion-pins of
hickory, and of the size that will work easy in two-inch
auger hole; clevis $\frac{3}{4}$ round iron with $\frac{1}{2}$-inch pins, see Fig.
168; slings, 3 feet 4 inches long, and 2 inches wide, they

Fig. 168—Foot Held by the Clevis.

should be made of very heavy leather, two thicknesses being stitched together, with iron clips at the ends to hold
the chains; the chains are 2 feet 6 inches long.   I use
heavy hickory sticks to wind up the rollers and hold them
in place.   The ratchet may be used, as shown in the cut,
if desired, but I prefer to allow the end of the winding stake
to strike against the cross-piece.   Use two-inch plank for
your floor.   This frame may look heavy, but it is necessary,
for they get terribly wrenched at times, and I should make
it heavier rather than lighter.—*By* LOTT PHILLIPS.

Ox Swing.

I enclose a plan for an ox swing that I am using, and
one that works well.   It is drawn to the scale of half an
an inch to the foot, which will enable anyone who desires

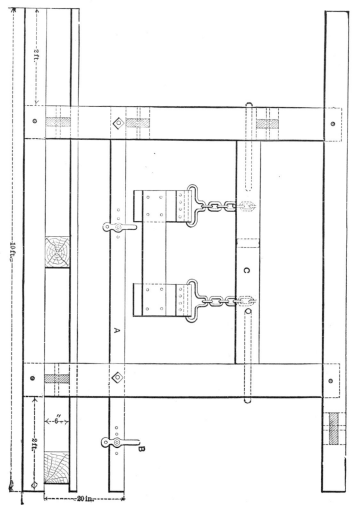

Fig. 169—Ox Swing. Side View.

to build one from the drawing I enclose. Fig. 169 is a side
view of the apparatus, and Fig. 170 the front. It is built
of lumber, six by eight inches, in sections. The floor is of
two-inch plank, raised one foot from the ground to prevent
stooping on the part of the operator. The nailing pieces, *A*

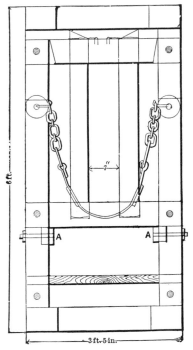

Fig. 170—End View.

are three by four inches, raised eight inches from the floor.

Each is furnished with two devices, *B*, for securing the
foot. They are let into the inside of the posts two-thirds of
their thickness, and are secured by bolts. The rollers, *C*,
are made of hard wood, six inches in diameter, and are

made to turn by means of levers. One of these might be framed into posts, if desired, and the other one alone made to turn. The belt, a detail of which is shown in Fig. 171, is made of strips of harness leather eight inches wide, riveted

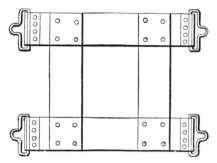

Fig. 171—Detail of Belt.

together with rings of half-inch iron, and a short chain to roll upon the rollers. The stanchions shown in Fig. 170 are made to open toward both sides, as there would not be sufficient room if they opened from only one side.—*By* G. E. F.

Making an Ox Frame.

The accompanying sketch, Fig. 172, of an ox frame will prove useful to a great many. My father used a frame like it for many years, and it suited him very well. In making it hardwood is essential. The dimensions of the timber are 8 in. x 11 in. There are three rollers, as indicated in the engraving by the letters *A*, *A* and *E*. The bars, *B*, when inserted in holes made for the purpose in the rollers, enable the smith to wind up the chains, *C*. At the right of the illustration is shown the clip for holding the ox's foot, and on each side of the frame and underneath the belt can be seen bars to which the clip is attached, by passing the clip pins through the holes in the bars and clips.—*By* T. C. B.

The Clip.

Fig. 172—Making an Ox Frame.

Swing for Shoeing Oxen.

Inclosed please find a description of an ox swing I built a few years ago, which shows for itself. If occasion requires we can shoe all four feet at the same time with no inconvenience to the ox, as he will lie in the straps and chew his cud as unconcerned as you please, unless he is a fractious " critter." In that case he will find himself in mid-air, kicking at what? Nothing, but having a fine country swing. In

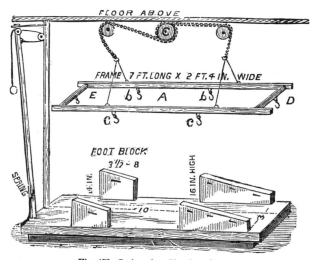

Fig. 173—Swing for Shoeing Oxen.

the old style of frame there is too much lumber to bruise himself against. I have often heard the remark from customers, with regard to the old frame, "I would rather my oxen would do a hard day's work, or even a week's work, than be shod;" and they were right.

When not in use the straps hang to the frame A, Fig. 173, by the hooks bb. You will see there is nothing for the ox to brace against to hurt himself, as each motion gives

him a swing.   He is attached to the frame and hangs simply by two chains from the main shaft, C, which goes across
the frame to the side of the shaft, and to which is attached
a large wheel to receive the rope for raising and lowering
by a windlass in front.   For fastening the feet I use straps
which go round the feet twice and buckle.   I have a head
rope to keep the ox forward.

The platform is 10 feet long by 3 feet wide, front of forward block 2 feet 6 in. from stanchion.   Block, 14½ in. at
the highest point by 9 in. wide and 4 in. thick, hollowed and
pitched toward the back ; also set on an angle, as the foot

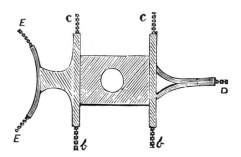

Fig. 174—Straps for Ox Swings.

will turn out when raised to the block.   From stanchions to
front of hind block, 6 feet.   To make the hind block, take
hard wood 3½ by 5 in., rabbit the lower inside two inches
deep, to receive the standards of plank, which are also cut
into the inside sill of platform, which is 6 by 6 ; give pitch
to suit the shoer.   The platform, from floor of shop to floor
of same, front, 1 foot 3 in., hind, 10 in., making a pitch of
5 in.

The straps, Fig. 174, from b to c, exclusive of chain, 4
feet ; from e to e, 4 feet ; from the strap, b c to d, 21 in. ;
from b c to b c, 3 feet, with brisket of same piece ; also the

bucket strap from *b* c, 15 in. ; chain at *d*, 8 in. ; ditto at *c*
and *b*, 15 in. ; at *e e*, 13 in. The above measures will make
each foot come right with the frame above, hung level 3
inches from stanchions. The hook at *c* to receive the chain
e 9 inches from front; for chain *b*, 22 in. from front; next *b*
2 feet from hind ; chain *d*, center of frame, hind.

The arranging of shaft above, raising and lowering the
ox, can be fitted to suit the place. The cost of whole, complete, will not be far from $50. Another important part is a
good head rope to keep the ox from swaying forward and
back.—*By* LUNK HEAD.

INDEX.

INDEX.

PRACTICAL BLACKSMITHING

New Work. **Just Out.**

Is a new book compiled from the practical articles which have appeared from time to time during the past few years in the columns of "THE BLACKSMITH AND WHEELWRIGHT."

Volume I. relates to **Ancient Blacksmithing,** and gives illustrations with descriptions of some ancient tools; tells how **Hammers Should Be Made;** and gives **Plans of Blacksmiths' Shops,** and a variety of plans of **Forges,** and the best way to build **Chimneys.** Illustrations and descriptions of a great variety of **Tongs, Hammers, Punches and Cold Chisels** are given.

Two prize articles on **Blacksmiths' Tools,** which have appeared in "THE BLACKSMITH AND WHEELWRIGHT," are printed in full.

There are five chapters in the book, each complete in itself.

Chapter I. treats of **Ancient and Modern Hammers.** Chapter II. **Ancient Tools.** Chapter III. **Chimneys, Forges, Fires, Shop Plans, Work Benches,** etc. Chapter IV. **Anvils and Anvil Tools.** Chapter V. **Blacksmiths' Tools**.

There is no book like it in the language: in fact, a work on blacksmithing has never before been published in this or any other country. As the publisher has decided to offer the work at a *low price*, with a view of *large sales*, the book is likely to find its way into the hands of all good blacksmiths wherever located. It will be sent *post-paid* to any part of the country on receipt of price, **$1.00.** Address, M. T. RICHARDSON, Publisher, 84 and 86 Reade Street, New York.

"GREENFIELD" FORGED OX SHOE.

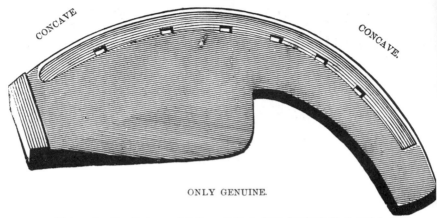

ONLY GENUINE.

Made under the Parker and Colburn Patents, from Burden's H. B. and S. Iron. Nail holes punched and every shoe perfect.

The Parker and Colburn Patents cover broadly the dies in which the shoes are forged. We are the *only* licensees, and all parties are cautioned against using either of the dies or the forging mechanism or processes so protected, as our rights under said patents will be fully maintained.

While we can furnish either the *Concave Shoe* with *One Calk*, or the *Flat Shoe* with *Two Calks*, we emphatically recommend the Concave, with one Calk, for the following reasons, viz.:

First—Because the entire bearing of the shoe should come upon the *shell* of the hoof and not upon the *ball* or the tender part of the foot, as is necessarily the case with the flat shoe. This principle is recognized by all experts in the shoeing both of oxen and horses, and will prevent a tendency to sore footedness.

Second—Because by having one Calk only the shoe can be cut off or lengthened and fitted more perfectly to the foot.

Third—Because by having one Calk only the shoer *can make the other calk at any angle he desires,*

No. 0, Full Length, Concave, 4½ inches, weight per set of eight shoes, 2 pounds.
" 1, " " " 5 " " " " 3 "
" 2, " " " 5½ " " " " 3½ "
" 3, " " " 6 " " " " 4 "
" 4, " " " 6½ " " " " 5 "

Packed in boxes or kegs of 100 pounds, half each rights and lefts. Full weight and no charge for packages.

PRICES.

For orders of One Ton, or more.................... .. ..9 cents per pound.
" 1,000 lbs. or more........... ....9¼ " "
" 500 " " ....10 " "
" Less than 500 lbs... ....10½ " "

Made ONLY by MILLERS FALLS COMPANY,
93 Reade Street, - - - New York.
SOLD BY ALL HARDWARE DEALERS.

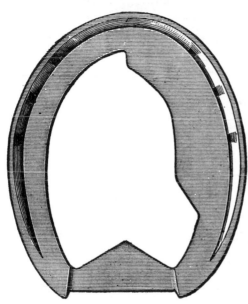